Let's Build Airplanes & Rockets!

 W9-BBC-461

10/99

Let's Build Airplanes & Rockets!

Dr. Ben P. Millspaugh & Dr. Beverley Taylor

Illustrations by Saundra Carmical

**LEARNING
TRIANGLE
PRESS**

*Connecting
kids, parents, and teachers
through learning*

An imprint of McGraw-Hill

**New York San Francisco Washington, D.C. Auckland Bogotá
Caracas Lisbon London Madrid Mexico City Milan
Montreal New Delhi San Juan Singapore
Sydney Tokyo Toronto**

McGraw-Hill

A Division of The McGraw·Hill Companies

©1996 by **The McGraw-Hill Companies, Inc.**
Published by Learning Triangle Press, an imprint of McGraw-Hill, Inc.

pbk 1 2 3 4 5 6 7 8 9 BBC/BBC 9 0 0 9 8 7 6

Elmer's Glue is a registered trademark of Borden Company. Scotch Tape is a registered trademark of 3M Company. Model Master is a registered trademark of Testor's Company. Product or brand names used in this book may be trade names or trademarks. Where we believe that there may be proprietary claims to such trade names or trademarks, the name has been used with an initial capital or it has been capitalized in the style used by the name claimant. Regardless of the capitalization used, all such names have been used in an editorial manner without any intent to convey endorsement of or other affiliation with the name claimant. Neither the author nor the publisher intends to express any judgment as to the validity or legal status of any such proprietary claims.

Library of Congress Cataloging-in-Publication Data
Millspaugh, Ben A.
    Let's build airplanes and rockets! / Ben P. Millspaugh & Beverley
Taylor.
        p.   cm.
    Includes bibliographical references and index.
    ISBN 0-07-042952-9
    1. Aeronautics—Popular works.   2. Aeronautics—History—Study and
teaching (Elementary)   3. Aeronautics—Experiments. I. Taylor,
Beverley.   II. Title.
TL546.7.M56   1996
629.1—dc20   96-22405
                                                           CIP

McGraw-Hill books are available at special quantity discounts to use as premiums and sales promotions, or for use in corporate training programs.
For more information, please write to the Director of Special Sales, McGraw-Hill, 11 West 19th Street, New York, NY 10011. Or contact your local bookstore.

Acquisitions editor: Judith Terrill-Breuer
Editorial team: Robert E. Ostrander, Executive Editor
               Sally Anne Glover, Book Editor
Production team: Katherine G. Brown, Director
               Donna K. Harlacher, Coding
               Toya B. Warner, Computer Artist
               Jeffrey Miles Hall, Computer Artist
               Brenda S. Wilhide, Computer Artist
               Wanda S. Ditch, Desktop Operator
               Linda L. King, Proofreader
               Jodi L. Tyler, Indexer
Design team: Jaclyn J. Boone, Designer   0429529
             Katherine Lukaszewicz, Associate Designer   LTP1

Contents

Introduction

Let's Build Airplanes & Rockets is for kids, parents, and teachers! The beauty of a bird in flight or the rumble of a jet flying overhead intrigues children and adults, and this fascination for flight—especially into space—can be used to enhance the learning of math, science, social studies, and language arts. Units on aviation and space can make children want to come to school. When children are studying about flight, whether it is in airplanes or spacecraft, they enjoy school more and want to learn more. It is a proven method, and it is called "aerospace education."

Parents also have found that a shared interest in aviation can go a long way in helping to strengthen family bonds. The history and related projects in this book are for children and parents. The "Classroom connections" sections aren't just for teachers either. Parents will find many ideas there for further reading and projects. You will find your children wanting to build more than one of each project as they get into investigating "what-will-happen-if" kinds of questions. The thinking skills children will be developing will carry over into their schoolwork and the rest of their lives.

Teachers will find a wealth of ideas for their classrooms in this book. Each "Classroom connections" section begins with a science lesson based on that chapter's project. This is followed by math, social studies, and language arts activities related to either the history or the model in that chapter. And don't just look at the chapter containing the model your students are building. Many of the "Classroom connections" ideas are applicable to other chapters as well. If you plan to use several models, be sure to look at the social studies sections of the first two chapters, which have ideas that can be carried on throughout the book. It's that fascination with flight that keeps the child interested, and teachers can turn this into learning in a variety of subjects.

America leads the world in aerospace technology, so let's instill that national pride in our young. These projects and the supporting text will give a "hands-on" visualization of the steps we've taken to reach the stars.

Note on materials needed

As these projects were designed, we worked hard to make sure that they used inexpensive and easy-to-obtain materials. Suggestions on where to obtain items are usually given in the materials list for each chapter. A few items are used in several chapters, so we decided to mention them here rather than each time they are used. Styrofoam meat trays of various sizes can usually be obtained free from your local supermarket butcher counter. Styrofoam eggs or cones can be purchased at most craft stores. The ones we used were manufactured by Flora Craft and were about $0.25 for eggs or $0.75 for cones (Fig. FM-1). Foam pipe insulation can be obtained from most building-supply centers for about $1.00 for a 5-foot section. If you are looking for it in the summer, you might have to check several places to find it in stock. In the winter, it is easy to find. Many of the projects are put together using a hot glue gun. Small hot glue guns can be purchased at most craft or department stores for about $5.00 (Fig. FM-2).

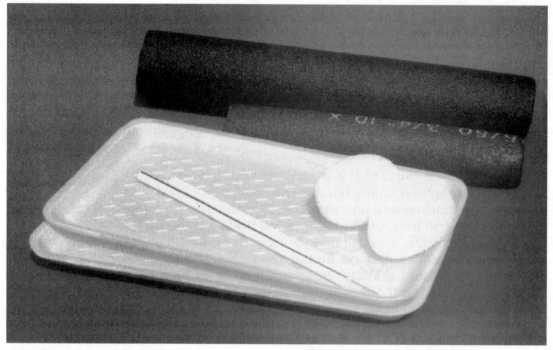

FM-1 *These are the basic materials you will need to make neat flying machines.*

A special note to teachers

Don't be surprised if you can't find understanding flight specifically mentioned in your school district's science curriculum. Neither is it in the recently released National Science Education Standards, nor is it in most state curriculum frameworks. That doesn't mean you can't make excellent use of the ideas in this book. A topic you will find emphasized in all of these various science curriculum guides is understanding motion and the forces that produce it. That's what this book is all about. If you have any doubts, read the "How they fly" chapter first.

The nature of scientific investigations, science as a human endeavor, and the history of science are also part of the national content standards. Middle-school students are expected to "develop a better understanding of scientific inquiry and the interactions between science and society." (NSES, p. 170.) Studying the history of the science of flight can let your students develop insights into the process of science in which the solution of a series of small problems finally leads to the larger goal. The newest breakthrough builds on

FM-2
*The secret to successfully building almost all of the projects in this book is the hot glue gun. It will bond plastic, foam, and balsa wood, and it only takes 60 seconds for the glue to set. **Be careful. The tip can burn you, so don't get careless.***

previous ones, and as much is learned from our failures as our successes. Many of the references provided allow your students to look deeper into the lives of the scientists and inventors who contributed to our understanding of flight and to look at connections to other historical events of the time. While each chapter focuses on someone who is well known in history, discussions and references encourage students to learn about the contributions of others who are not so well known—particularly women and African-Americans. So, you see, you won't have any trouble figuring how the science and history of flight fits into your curriculum, even though you can't find the word "flight" in it anywhere.

The beginning of manned flight

1

Kites, 500 B.C.

The wonderful kite has been around for more than 2,000 years. Historians say that kites originated in the Far East. While we don't know for sure when the first kite was made or who made it, we do know that the first written record of one was made in China about 500 B.C.

The Chinese used kites for religious events and entertainment. It is also recorded that kites were first used in warfare for signaling purposes. The Japanese were great kite builders, and there is evidence that they were the first to build a kite capable of carrying a human being. Kites also were used by the military for observing their enemies.

Kites were brought to the West in the early fourteenth century. One military application in the West was for dropping "firebombs" on enemy positions. The kite, it might be said, was the first "bomber."

For sport, the Japanese developed the art of kite "fighting." These kites were very maneuverable, and the object of the competition was to disable an opponent by cutting the control lines.

One of the most famous events in scientific history happened in 1752 when Benjamin Franklin used a kite to "catch" electricity. Although it was extremely dangerous, Franklin was able to prove that lightning was a form of electricity. During the years following Benjamin Franklin's experiments, kites became very popular, and many were used for both scientific and military experiments.

Early in the nineteenth century, a British schoolteacher, George Pocock, made large kites that were used to pull a horseless carriage. He claimed that one was used to lift and fly his daughter, Martha. Another Englishman, George Cayley, used a kite to lift a glider. You'll learn more about him in chapter 3.

In 1893, Lawrence Hargrave, an Australian, invented the box kite. This design was used by many aviation pioneers, including Octave Chanute. Chanute was a railroad builder who used his knowledge of bridge structure to develop very strong box kites. This technology was later used by the Wright brothers to strengthen their two-winged (biplane) gliders and the Wright Flyer.

Some parachutes now use a form of kite technology. The Jalbert "parafoil" has a canopy that looks like a wing. The leading and trailing edges of the canopy open to form a large wing that literally flies the jumper to the ground. This allows the individual to land slowly and with great control.

Aviation historians consider the kite to be the first successful craft capable of human-carrying flight. Kites are easy to make and can be a source of great excitement for everyone.

Fast facts

❏ It is believed that the Chinese developed the first kite as early as 1000 B.C.

❏ In 1740, the temperature of clouds was recorded with a thermometer attached to a kite flown by two Scots.

❏ A kite was once used to carry a cable across a gorge on the Niagara River.

❏ Flat kites need a tail for balance.

❏ Kites have been used for photography and military observation.

❏ Kites are now being used to pull people on surfboards.

❏ Japanese families celebrate the birth of children by flying kites.

❏ Many countries in the Far East hold kite-fighting competitions in which teams try to entangle and cut their opponents' kites.

❏ Nonrigid kites (such as the sled kite described in this chapter) are a modern invention.

Project 1

You build it—
A simple sled kite

There are hundreds of kite designs that will fly if built properly. The sled kite, described here, is easy to build in less than an hour. With just a little wind, you're up and flying in no time, and it is great fun!

A. The basic materials

1. Two 24-inch wooden dowels (about ¼ inch in diameter) or bamboo strips.

2. Spool or roll of strong, lightweight cotton or kite string.

3. A sheet of plastic kite material or similar light, strong plastic sheet. (Possibilities are heavy-duty garbage bags, drop cloths sold in building supply stores, or mylar found in party supply stores.)

4. Plastic strapping tape—the kind used for wrapping packages.

5. Strips of ribbon or crepe paper (optional).

B. Tools

1. Scissors to cut string and plastic.

C. Safety precautions

1. Always be careful when cutting with scissors.

2. Always fly your kite in a large, open area away from power lines, telephone lines, and trees.

D. Steps of construction

1. Cut two wooden strips each 24 inches long.

2. Cut the plastic sail material to the dimensions shown in Fig. 1-1 (one big piece, not three separate ones).

3. Tape the wooden strips into position, as shown in Fig. 1-1.

4. For strength, make sure you reinforce the top and bottom of the wooden pieces with the strapping tape.

5. Cut two pieces of cord, each 10 feet long.

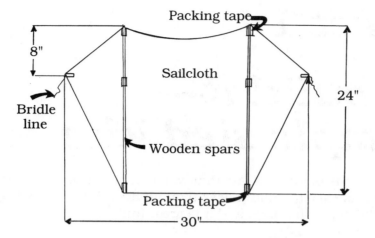

1-1 Build your sled kite to these dimensions.

6. Using the packing tape, secure one end of each piece of string to the pointed edges of the sail, as shown in Fig. 1-1. These pieces of cord make up the "bridle." Eventually the string or cord you will use to fly your kite is attached to this bridle. The bridle should be roughly five times the vertical length of your kite.

7. Strips of ribbon or crepe paper can be used for tails. These ribbons are taped to the ends of the sticks. This kite needs no tail, but it adds visual excitement to the flight.

8. If you want to decorate the kite, do so at this point. Markers or simple acrylic paints can be used to make fascinating designs. Note that the sticks will be on the outside of the sail, so decorate the inside face.

9. Tie the ends of the bridle together. (See Fig. 1-2.) Tie the cord used to fly the kite to this knot (or all three cords could be tied to a small metal ring).

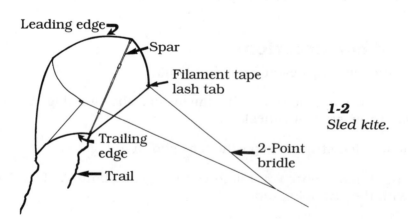

1-2 Sled kite.

E. Flying your kite

1. Stand with your back to the wind. Hold your kite in one hand, and hold the string or spool in the other. Release the kite while maintaining tension in the string. The wind will catch the sail and lift the kite. Slowly let out more line. Tugging on the kite might help the kite gain altitude.

2. In light or erratic winds, you might want to use a partner to help with the launch. Have your partner hold the kite about 30 feet downwind from you. Pull out a little extra slack string. At your signal, have your partner gently toss the kite upward as you back up or pull in line.

3. If the kite starts to drop in the air while flying, step back or wind in the line, and the kite will rise again.

F. Investigations

1. After you have practiced with your kite for awhile, try making some changes in your kite to see what effect there is on its flight. Fly your kite with and without a tail. The instructions say you don't need a tail, but does it change anything? Try retying your tow line at a different point on the bridal so that the bridal is no longer symmetrical. Will your kite still fly?

2. Make a second kite with different dimensions. Try making it taller or wider. Does this affect how it flies? Get a friend or parent to help you so you can fly both kites at once. Do they fly at the same height? Do they fly with the same angle between the kite and the wind?

3. Be sure to read about kites in "How they fly," chapter 11.

Also recommended

More project ideas!

1. *Into the Wind* kite catalog. From *Into the Wind*, 1408 Pearl Street, Boulder, CO 80302. Phone 1-800-541-0314 or Fax 303-449-7315.

    "Into The Wind" is one of the premier kite stores in the nation. The company has a wonderful catalog that is free by writing, calling, or faxing a request to the numbers given. Teachers, Dr. Ben says . . . if you find you're interested in kites, this store has everything.

2. *American KITE* magazine. *American KITE* is published quarterly and runs $14 for an annual subscription.

    If interested, write American Kite, P.O. Box 699, Cedar Ridge, CA 95924. If you want to call, their number is 916-273-3855 or Fax 916-273-3319. This is an excellent magazine all about kites. It has articles about kites, plans for building kites, and advertising from manufacturers from around the world. This is an outstanding resource for teachers.

3. Itsy Bitsy Kite. From Kite Sails, 3555 Jubliant Place, Colorado Springs, CO 80917. Phone is 719-596-2332.

    This kite is only 6 inches tall and has a ribbon tail that is about 24 inches long. It can be flown in the house, or it will trail you down the hall

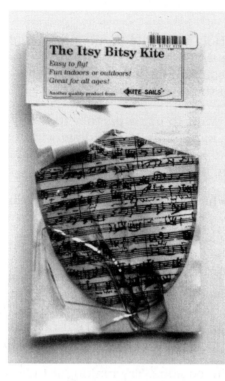

1-3
Imagine walking down the hallway at school with a kite flying behind you. You can do it with this recommended project, "The Itsy Bitsy Kite!"

at school. It has a tiny spool of thread for its flying line and comes in several designs. You'll love this little guy! (See Fig. 1-3.)

Classroom connections

A. Science

1. Just getting the kite made can be a lesson in measurement. After you have made the kites and flown them, discuss any observations the students might have made about the way the kites fly. Discuss how the forces of the wind, gravity, and the string combine to keep the kite in the air. (See "How they fly," chapter 11, for a discussion of these forces.) Be sure to stress the importance of Newton's Third Law of motion to the flight of the kite.

2. Divide the class into small groups and have each group make a sled kite with different dimensions. Have some groups keep the same aspect ratio (width divided by length) while changing the size of the kite. Have other groups change the aspect ratio by changing either the width or the length of the kite. Groups will then fly their kites and compare performance. Which fly highest? Which are most stable? Are some easier to launch than others? Do all the ones with the same aspect ratio behave the same? In general, kites with a large aspect ratio fly high but are not very stable, while kites with a low aspect ratio are usually stable but are more likely to fly low. Encourage students to hypothesize what causes the differences in the way the kites fly. (Figs. 1-4 and 1-5.)

3. More kite activities can be found in the National Science Teachers Association book, *Flights of Imagination: An Introduction to Aerodynamics*, by Wayne Hoskings.

1-4 Kite shops are colorful, fun places to visit.

*1-5
Sarah Good, of
Breckinridge, Colorado,
helps her father manage
their kite shop, "Flying
Colors."*

4. With younger students, you might want to connect the kites to previous studies of their senses. Which of your five senses (touching, seeing, smelling, hearing, tasting) would you use to fly a kite? Write the senses as a heading on a blank piece of paper. Under each heading, list words and phrases to indicate how a specific sense would be connected to kite flying.

B. Mathematics

1. Almost all kites have a symmetric shape. Review the concept of symmetry with your students. Have them look around the room for symmetric objects. Collect some simple line drawings such as might be found in a preschool coloring book. Have the students place a mirror perpendicular to the paper at different places on the drawing to see the various symmetrical shapes that are produced. Use the mirrors to find the number of lines of symmetry that can be found in various geometric shapes, such as triangles, rectangles, and octagons. Have students draw symmetric shapes with the aid of a piece of colored Plexiglas. When drawing symmetric shapes, it is very difficult to make both halves exactly alike. The colored Plexiglas, which acts as a partially reflecting mirror, solves this problem. First draw one side of your figure. Now set the Plexiglas on the edge of the drawing that is to be the line of symmetry. Looking through the mirror from the drawing side, you will see a reflection of your drawing on the blank side of the paper. Trace this reflection on the paper. The neat thing about these mirrors is that you can see through them and see your hand and pencil while you trace the reflection. Plexiglas devices meant for this purpose are called Miras and are available from companies that sell math manipulatives, such as Cuisenaire (800-237-0338). A toy called a Reflect-a-Sketch does the same thing. Almost any colored Plexiglas will work, so you could just buy a large sheet and cut it up.

2. Discuss aspect ratios with your students. A square has an aspect ratio of one. Rectangles that are tall and skinny or short and long have very large or very small aspect ratios. Select some objects around the room, measure their width and height, and compute their aspect ratio. Have the students work in pairs to compute their own aspect ratios. It is best to agree on some point like the shoulders for measuring width so that everyone does the same thing.

C. Social studies

1. On the world map in your classroom, attach a small kite to the country of China, identifying China's significance in the history of the kite. Continue this project as you make other models from this book.

2. Research other achievements of the early Chinese, such as the discovery of magnetism, the prediction of eclipses, and the writing of the first dictionary. Older students will be fascinated by *The Genius of China: 3,000 Years of Science, Discovery and Invention*, by Robert Temple. Inside the front and back covers of this book is a chart listing 100 inventions, the time of their first use in China, and the time lag between then and their adoption in the West.

3. Make a timeline of the history of China. Include the invention of the kite somewhere between 1000 and 500 B.C. An excellent source of information for your timeline is *World History Dates* by Jane Chisholm, which is part of the Usborne Illustrated World History Series.

4. Compile a list of other interesting world events in the same time period as the invention of the kite. For instance, the city of Troy fell to Greek warriors

who entered the city inside a huge wooden horse in 1190 B.C. King Solomon ordered the building of the temple in Jerusalem in 973 B.C. Rome was founded around 750 B.C. In India about 528 B.C., the religion of Buddhism was established. The Usborne book previously mentioned and the *Smithsonian Visual Timeline of Inventions* are good references for this project.

D. Language arts

1. Write step-by-step directions for flying a kite. Imagine that you are teaching someone who has no knowledge of kite flying. It is important to include all of the steps, or the kite won't fly. Tell about the safety measures involved in flying a kite. You might want to work with a partner on this activity.

2. Read about what life was like in ancient China. Two good books for middle-school students are *The Ancient Chinese*, by Lai Po Kan, and *The Ancient Far East*, by Yonit and Alastair Percival.

3. Imagine yourself lying on your back and watching a kite fly overhead. Brainstorm a list of words that describe what you see. Does everyone see the same thing? Is one person's description necessarily better than another person's? Read your list of descriptive words to a classmate.

4. Here are some ideas for class discussions:

   a. When the Chinese developed the first kites, they did it for fun and family entertainment. Talk with a partner and try to imagine what you might have done 600 or 700 years ago for entertainment. What did children play with? What kinds of toys could they have made for themselves?

   b. What does your family enjoy doing together? Does everyone enjoy the same activities, or do family members sometimes agree to try something new to them?

   c. This book is based on beginnings and on people who took chances to develop the ideas they had. Do you remember the first time you wanted to begin a new activity? Maybe it was piano lessons or skiing. How did you feel? Were you nervous about measuring up to everyone's expectations? After you worked at the skill for a while, did it become easier?

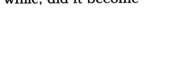

First powered free-flight by humans

2

Montgolfier balloon, 1783

Two brothers, Joseph Michel (1740–1810) and Jacques Etienne (1745–1799) Montgolfier, were born and lived in a small French town named Annonay. They worked on developing lighter-than-air craft for several years before they launched a balloon carrying humans.

They thought about a lifting force when they observed bits of paper being carried upward in a fireplace. They started experimenting by holding the open ends of bags over a fire and were excited when the bags would float upward. They were convinced that they had found a magic lifting force and later named it "Montgolfier gas."

Their first balloon was made of paper and linen. It was about 35 feet wide and flew for ¾ of a mile from its launch point. On November 21, 1783, two Frenchmen, Pilatre de Rozier and the Marquis d'Arlandes, made the first human-carrying free-flight in a Montgolfier balloon. The craft was about seven stories tall and climbed to an estimated 3,000 feet in altitude. It drifted across the city of Paris and eventually landed in an area between two mill houses. One of the problems encountered in this epic flight was fire. The "aeronauts," as they were called, put out the flames using sponges.

Ballooning soon became popular, especially with wealthy aristocrats. The popularity spread to America, and on January 9, 1793, French aeronaut Jean-Pierre Blanchard made the first balloon flight in America. He carried a letter from President George Washington.

First powered free-flight by humans

Fast facts

❏ Joseph Montgolfier lived from 1740–1810.
❏ Jacques Montgolfier lived from 1745–1799. (Fig. 2-1.)

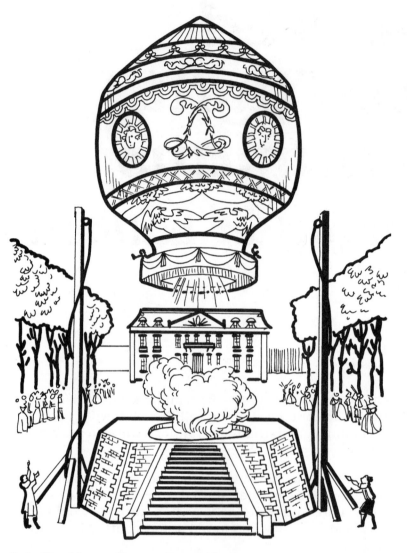

2-1 *The Montgolfier Balloon, the first powered free-flight by humans—1783.*

❏ The father of the Montgolfier brothers owned a paper factory. His boys observed a paper bag floating upward on a hot air current from a fire. They wondered if they could find a way to make this bag carry weight. In their early balloon experiments, the Montgolfier brothers used straw, old shoes, and rotten meat for fuel.
❏ They demonstrated their invention to King Louis XVI and Marie Antoinette of France in September of 1783. As part of this demonstration, they put a duck, a rooster, and a sheep on board. These animals became the first free-

flight passengers in history. The balloon flew for 8 minutes and went nearly 2 miles.

❏ On November 21, 1783, Jean Pilatre de Rozier and Marquis d'Arlandes made the first manned free-flight in history.

❏ When early balloonists landed in the French countryside, they found frightened farmers confronting them with pitchforks. To calm the farmers, aeronauts offered the farmers wine or champagne as a "peace offering." The tradition continues to this day. Balloon flights usually end with a champagne celebration for pilot, passengers, and chase crews.

❏ The French army was the first to use balloons to observe enemy troop activity.

❏ America had balloons in the Civil War. An American by the name of Thaddeus Lowe commanded the first balloon operation. He was arrested several times by Confederate soldiers for being a spy.

First powered free-flight by humans

Project 2

You build it— A Montgolfier hot-air balloon

You are going to be making a hot-air balloon that will fly indoors. The heated air inside the balloon will make it rise in the surrounding air. The cooler the air around the balloon, the better it flies. It takes a long time for the hair dryer to get the air warm enough to make the balloon start to float. Be patient. The colder the room around the balloon, the better.

A. The basic materials

See Fig. 2-2.

1. Plastic dry-cleaner protective bag.

2. 6–8 paper clips.

3. A roll of common household transparent tape.

4. A sheet of newspaper or butcher paper.

2-2 *To make your hot-air balloon, you will need these components: a cleaner bag, tape, paper clips, and a hair dryer.*

B. Tools

1. A hair dryer.

2. Scissors.

3. An iron used to press laundry.

C. Safety precautions

1. Don't get the balloon too hot or the plastic will melt.

2. Keep plastic bags away from small children. They can cause suffocation if placed over the head.

D. Steps of construction

1. The cleaner plastic bags come on a roll and are perforated so they can easily be separated from the roll. Hot air will leak through these perforations unless sealed. Plug in your iron and turn the heat up to the "synthetic" setting.

2. Using scissors, cut the plastic bag just below the perforations.

3. Lay the plastic bag out on a table top. Put the plastic bag between two newspaper sheets. (See Fig. 2-3.)

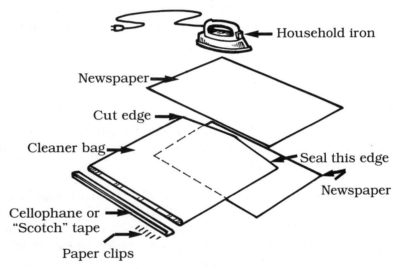

2-3 *Sealing the cleaner bag.*

4. Carefully seal the edge you cut by rubbing the iron over the newspaper on top of the edge.

5. When the plastic has cooled, check to make sure that it has a complete seal.

6. The bottom edge of the balloon must be strengthened and slightly weighted by applying a line of tape around the entire edge. Don't add any more weight than necessary.

7. Your balloon is almost ready. Put your four to six paper clips equally spaced around the bottom where you've taped. This will add just enough weight to balance the balloon and keep it in the right position during flight.

First powered free-flight by humans

E. Flying your balloon

1. Get a friend to help hold the balloon while you heat the air inside of it with the hair dryer. Once the balloon fills, it will give indications that it wants to fly. If it gently settles to the floor, remove some of the weight by removing two paper clips. If it still wants to settle, wait for a cooler time of day. Happy flying!

F. Investigations

1. Observe your balloon carefully as it inflates. What changes do you notice taking place?

2. Experiment with the number of paper clips on the bottom. What is the smallest number that will work? What is the largest number?

3. Why is it important to have the paper clips evenly spaced? Put more on one side than the other. What happens when you try to fly the balloon?

4. Save your hot-air balloon and try flying it on another day when the house is either warmer or cooler. Can you observe any difference in the way the balloon behaves?

Also recommended

More project ideas!

1. A paper hot-air balloon kit. From Space Age Distributing Company, 4888 Cedar Ridge N.E. Grand Rapids, MI 49595. This could be a fun project for gifted elementary students.

2. *Aerospace Education Catalog*. From the Civil Air Patrol Supply Depot, 14400 Airport Blvd., Amarillo, TX 79111. 1-800-335-2001. This catalog is especially recommended for teachers and has 45 pages of aviation and space-related projects, kits, toys, books, and much more. Teachers, take it from Dr. Ben, this is one great catalog!

3. For information about balloons, contact The Lighter Than Air Society, 1800 Triplet Blvd., Akron, OH 44306, or the Balloon Federation of America, 806 15th St. N.W., Suite 610, Washington, DC 20005.

Classroom connections

A. Science

1. Have students perform the investigations described at the end of the project instructions. In a class discussion, have the students report their results and any other observations they might have made. Also discuss any difficulties they might have had, what caused them, and how they corrected them.

2. Be sure to discuss the role density plays in the flight of the balloon. See "How they fly" in chapter 11 for a discussion of why the balloon rises. You might want to demonstrate for your students that air expands when it is

warmed. An easy way to do this is to place a balloon over the mouth of a plastic bottle. Put the bottle into a bucket of hot water. As the air inside the bottle warms, it will expand, inflating the balloon. If you move the bottle to a bucket of cold water, it will deflate again.

3. Edmund Scientific sells a solar hot-air balloon that is basically a large black plastic bag that one partially fills with air and leaves in strong sunlight. As the air in the bag warms up, it expands, decreasing the density of the bag-air system. It will slowly rise in the air as it warms. Purchase one of these and allow your class to fly it on a cool, sunny day. Discuss the similarities and differences in the way the open system you made with the dry-cleaning bags and the closed black-bag system work. (Edmund Scientific, 1-609-547-8880, Solar Air Shuttle, Item #H39804, $4.95.)

B. Mathematics

1. The Montgolfier brothers' first hot-air balloon inflated to about 100 feet in circumference. Encourage students to brainstorm a list of objects they estimate to be about 100 feet in circumference. Measure out 100 feet of yarn or string. Tie the ends together. In a gymnasium or out on the playground, have each class member grasp a section of the string with both hands and move back until a circle is formed. Discuss the objects students originally estimated would be about 100 feet in circumference during their brainstorming session. How realistic were their ideas? This activity will give students a visual appreciation for sizes and the meaning of circumference. Remember to reuse the string!

2. Combine math and art by having students use an X-Y coordinate system to draw a hot-air balloon. Provide ½-inch or 1-cm grid graph paper for the students. Instruct the students to plot the points in Table 2-1 on their graph paper.

Table 2-1 Coordinates.

x	y
1	11
1	17
4	20
12	20
15	17
15	11
11	8
10	5
10	2
6	2
6	5
5	8

Connect the dots to form the outline of a hot-air balloon (see Fig. 2-4). Students who get unusual shapes should check for misplotted points. After completing their graphs, students can create colorful designs for their hot-air balloons. The finished product will look nicer if you use graph paper with pale blue lines.

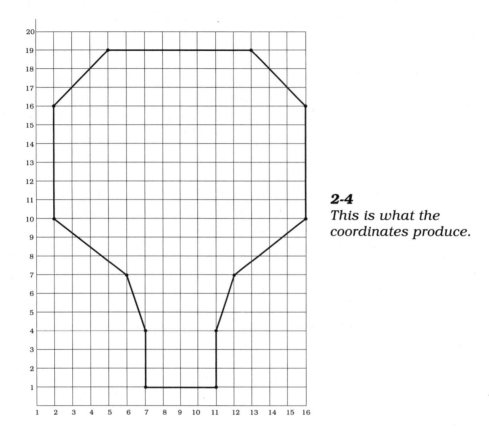

2-4
This is what the coordinates produce.

C. Social studies

1. If you plan to use several of the projects in this book in your classroom, you might want to create a timeline above the blackboard or in the hall. Use something like adding-machine tape to make the timeline. You will need to cover from about 1780 to 1960. Select a scale appropriate for the amount of space you have, such as 1 foot represents 10 years. Write the date on the tape every 10 or 20 years. As you make the models, copy the picture on the first or second page of the chapter and place it under the appropriate date. You might want to enlarge it and let one of your students color it first. Under the picture, put an information card with the person's achievements.

2. Research life in France in 1783. Try to imagine what the life of a typical person was like. Write about what you would have thought if you had been there in 1783 and looked up and saw this contraption flying overhead. Or imagine that you are the first human to fly free, as did de Rozier and d'Arlandes in 1783. Describe what you saw as you looked across the French countryside. What kind of crops were grown? Was it all farmland? Were there cities or factories?

3. Continue your studies of France by reading about the events and issues that led up to the French Revolution in 1789. Or read about French involvement in the American Revolution, which was ended by the Treaty of Paris just a few months before the de Rozier and d'Arlandes' flight. Junior-high students will find a concise history of the era in *History's Timeline: A 40,000 Year Chronology of Civilization* by Cooke, Kramer, and Rowland-Entwistle. Having an overview that can be read quickly will encourage students to pick out one or two events to research in more detail.

D. Language arts

1. Younger students will enjoy reading *The Flying Balloon* by Cyriel Verleyen. Middle-school students can read about the Montgolfier brothers and other early balloonists in *Pioneers of Flight* by Brian Williams.

2. Choose one of the animals (duck, rooster, or sheep) from the second flight of a Montgolfier balloon. Pretend you are this animal and write a first-person account of the flight. How did you feel flying over land? What did you see? Did the appearance of the hot-air balloon surprise people on the ground?

3. Here are some possibilities for class discussions:
   a. Travel was very restricted in the days of the Montgolfier brothers. Many people did not even leave their villages. How would your life be different if you had never left your hometown? What are the advantages of being able to leave your hometown? Does it change your opinion of the world and its people?
   b. Are you a brave spirit? In your opinion, what qualities make a brave spirit? Discuss how you think most explorers felt when they were making new discoveries. Were the first balloonists brave spirits?

The first modern airplane -shaped aircraft

Sir George Cayley, 1804

Sir George Cayley was an Englishman, and he developed the first modern "airplane" shape. He is also known as the "Father of Aerial Navigation." George was knighted by the King of England and thus earned the title "Sir" (Fig. 3-1).

He developed many of his ideas about flight from watching birds gliding in the air. He noticed that some birds didn't flap their wings, yet they continued to soar high in the sky. He used his observations to build theories about how humans could fly with machines.

Using his theories, Cayley began experimenting with wings on different models. Some of his models were very similar to the airplanes we have today. One of his models was a triplane (an aircraft with three wings), which was actually a kite shaped like a diamond. The tail of this model had

3-1 *George Cayley's Glider: The first modern airplane-shaped aircraft.*

vertical and horizontal stabilizers, or small winglike surfaces. Most of today's airplanes have vertical and horizontal stabilizers. Sir George was "ahead of his time." He had ideas about flight and aircraft long before anyone else.

He devoted most of his adult life to experimenting and developing ideas related to aviation. Four years before his death, he was experimenting on a glider with wings and bicycle wheels.

Fast facts

❏ Sir George Cayley was born December 27, 1773, and died in 1857.

❏ He was a boy when the Montgolfier balloon flew.

❏ He studied chemistry and electricity in college.

❏ In 1810, at the age of 36, Cayley published three scientific reports in the *Journal of Natural Philosophy* about his experiments. Later scientists used these experiments to base research on modern aerodynamics.

❏ He invented the caterpillar tractor, automatic signals for railroad crossings, and a self-righting lifeboat.

❏ Sir George Cayley used theories of mathematics to explain his ideas about flight.

❏ Sir Cayley was never able to experience flying, but his work enabled others to do so.

Project 3

You build it— Cayley's glider

For a long time, children have been building model airplanes from balsa because it is a light, strong wood. During World War II, the British wood industry produced an airplane made of balsa wood sandwiched in between plywood. It was known as the DeHavilland Mosquito, and it was a very successful fighter-bomber.

This unit introduces children, teachers, and parents to basic gliders. A nice little flying machine can be made using either balsa wood or soda straws and meat-tray foam. A hot glue gun is recommended for bonding either the balsa or plastic surfaces. Most small hot glue guns can be purchased at craft stores for under $5.95. Experiment to your heart's content. Keep trying, and you'll eventually build a great little flyer.

Instructions for an even easier paper glider are given in Fig. 3-2. This model allows you to experiment with the control surfaces, rudders, and ailerons (Fig. 3-3) described in chapter 11, "How they fly." You can control the flight of your glider in ways very similar to those that a pilot uses to control a real plane.

A. The basic materials

1. For fuselage, use a ⅛-inch-×-¼-inch-×-12-inch balsa strip or a plastic soda straw.

2. For the wings and tail, use a ¹⁄₁₆-inch-×-4-inch-×-12-inch sheet of balsa wood or a Styrofoam meat tray with at least 8 inches of flat surface in its length.

3. For front weight, use modeling clay, putty, a small food-bag clip, or other small weights.

A ¹⁄₁₆-inch-×-4-inch-×-36-inch balsa sheet can be purchased from hobby stores or from Midwest Model Company Products, School Division, 400 S. Indiana St., Hobart, IN, 46342. The sheet used in the Cayley project cost $2.00 and was purchased locally. The ⅛-inch-×-¼-inch-×-36-inch balsa strip was purchased locally for $.50.

B. Tools

1. Scissors to cut out balsa or foam wing and tail pieces.

2. Hot glue gun to bond components together.

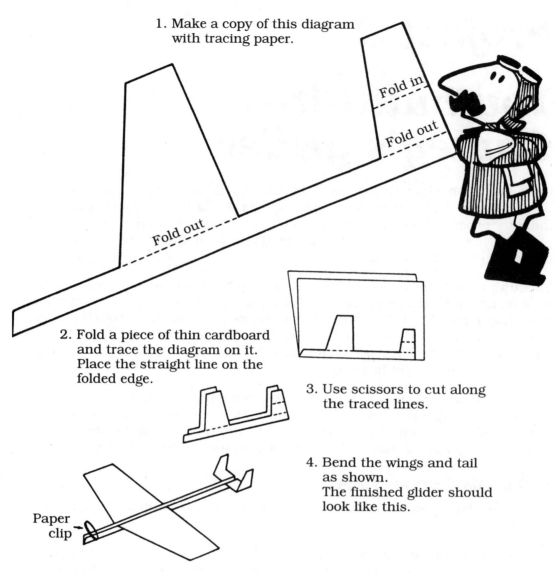

1. Make a copy of this diagram with tracing paper.

Fold in

Fold out

Fold out

2. Fold a piece of thin cardboard and trace the diagram on it. Place the straight line on the folded edge.

3. Use scissors to cut along the traced lines.

4. Bend the wings and tail as shown. The finished glider should look like this.

Paper clip

3-2 *A simple glider!*

C. Safety precautions

1. Always be careful when cutting with scissors.

2. Hot glue guns can burn you if you get careless. Don't get in a hurry, and be sure to unplug it when you're through.

3. Never sail the glider towards someone. Use an open area like a playground or a park to launch your glider.

D. Steps of construction

1. Make a copy of the template page (Fig. 3-4) on a copy machine. This will save the book from damage. Cut out the templates and use them as patterns to cut out the wings, fin, and horizontal stabilizer from the balsa wood sheet or Styrofoam.

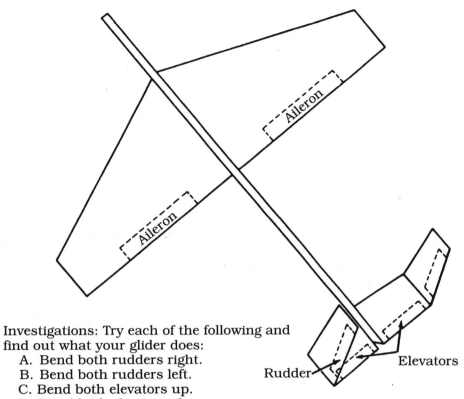

Investigations: Try each of the following and
find out what your glider does:
    A. Bend both rudders right.
    B. Bend both rudders left.
    C. Bend both elevators up.
    D. Bend both elevators down.
    E. Bend the right aileron up and the left aileron down.
    F. Bend the right aileron down and the left aileron up.
What conclusions can you draw from the results of these activities?

3-3 *Making a glider.*

2. The wings are glued to the body or "fuselage" (balsa or soda straw) about 2 inches in back of the nose.

3. The horizontal stabilizer is glued to the tail end of the fuselage. Make sure that the stabilizer is exactly parallel to the wing.

4. The vertical fin is hot-glued to the stabilizer. Make sure that it is perpendicular to the stabilizer (Fig. 3-5).

5. Add something to the nose for weight. Hot glue can be used to attach small weights, although using clay makes for easier adjustments.

E. Flying your glider

1. Find a large, open area so you won't hit anyone or get your glider lodged in a tree or bush.

2. Hold the glider level and give it a gentle push (Fig. 3-6).

3. If the nose is too light, it will pitch up and stall, then flutter to the ground. If the nose is too heavy, it will dive. Generally speaking, nose weight is the key to successful flight.

4. Keep experimenting until it sails just right . . . then happy flying.

The first modern airplane-shaped aircraft

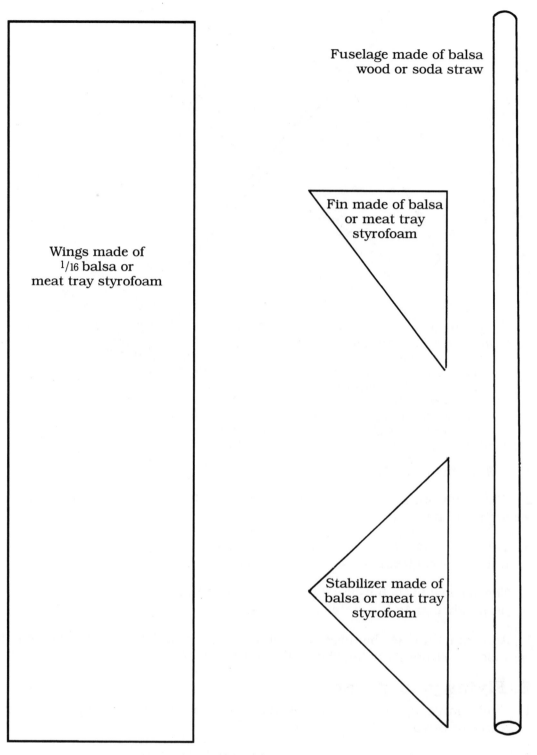

Fuselage made of balsa
wood or soda straw

Fin made of balsa
or meat tray
styrofoam

Wings made of
$1/16$ balsa or
meat tray styrofoam

Stabilizer made of
balsa or meat tray
styrofoam

3-4 *Cayley glider template.*

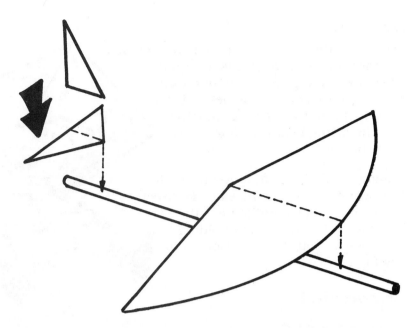

3-5 *To assemble your Cayley glider, first cut out the parts and then hot-glue them in the position shown.*

3-6
Jennifer tried the Cayley glider with a nose weight made of modeling clay. The glider flew quite well.

F. Investigations

1. Experiment with different amounts of nose weight. As you increase the nose weight, is it a gradual change or sudden change from the pitch up and stall behavior to a smooth glide? Is there a range of weights that will give a smooth glide before the diving behavior of too much weight begins?

2. Hold the plane lightly by a wing tip and let it dangle. Note what part of the fuselage is directly under your thumb. This point is near the center of gravity of the glider. Try holding your glider there as you throw it. Does this improve its flight?

Also recommended

More project ideas!

1. Flip Glider and Star Glider. From Midwest Products, Inc., School Division, 400 S. Indiana St., P.O. Box 64, Hobart, IN 46342.

2. Teachers can get "Class-Paks" of the Flip Glider and Star Glider from the Civil Air Patrol Supply Depot. The depot has hundreds of aerospace education supplies for teachers. Request their catalog by calling 1-800-858-4370.

3. There is a company called Pitsco that offers a huge inventory of aerospace education supplies. They have a wonderful catalog of gliders, other models, classroom aids, kits, toys, books, and just about everything to enhance the curriculum. Write PITSCO, P.O. Box 1708, Pittsburgh, KS 66762. Their telephone number is 1-800-835-0686. Dr. Ben says . . . this is one tremendous catalog for teachers. You gotta have this one!

Classroom connections

A. Science

1. Have your class make the paper airplane shown in Fig. 3-2 and carry out the investigations described in Fig. 3-3. Experimenting should be done in a large, open space such as the gym or cafeteria. Be sure the students notice the difference between the effects of the ailerons and the rudders, both of which turn the airplane. When the rudders are used, the airplane maintains a fairly level flight while turning. When the ailerons are used, the airplane banks or rolls tilting to one side. The elevators raise and lower the nose of the plane. Raising the elevators increases the force of the air on the back of the plane and causes the tail to drop and the nose to rise.

Name	Estimation (in feet)	Actual (in feet)	Difference (in feet)

3-7 Cayley's glider contest: Data collection sheet.

2. If your students are interested in pursuing the science of paper airplanes further, *How to Make and Fly Paper Airplanes* by Ralph Barnaby (retired Air Force Captain) is an excellent resource. This book begins by dropping a sheet of paper and looking at air resistance and stability, then it gradually has the reader make changes to the sheet of paper and see what happens. One is lead through many steps, with nice discussions of the science involved along the way, until one finally has a paper airplane. The last chapter even covers how to make loops, circles, and S-turns.

The first modern airplane-shaped aircraft

20										
19										
18										
17										
16										
15										
14										
13										
12										
11										
10										
9										
8										
7										
6										
5										
4										
3										
2										
1										

Name

Estimations ☐   Actual ☐

3-8 *Cayley's glider contest: Sample setup for class graph.*

3. Connie Rodgers and Karen Deike, our elementary education consultants, also recommend the computer software "The Greatest Paper Airplanes" by Mindscape. This program presents 25 different airplanes you can fold and fly. If your local computer store doesn't stock the software, you can get it directly from Kittyhawk Software Co., 60 Leveronis Ct., Novato, CA 94949, (415) 883-3000.

B. Mathematics

1. After completion of Cayley gliders, plan a contest. Students will mark off 20 feet, in 1-foot increments, down a hallway or outdoors using masking tape. Use a black marker to write the number of feet from the starting line on each piece of masking tape. Each student will estimate the distance he or she feels the glider will travel and record the prediction on the data collection sheet (Fig. 3-7). Taking turns, students will fly their gliders with other students measuring and recording the actual distance each one traveled. The contest winner is not the person whose glider went the greatest distance, but rather the one whose estimate was closest to the actual flight.

2. Compile all estimates and actual distances flown, creating a double bar graph to display in the hallway. Use butcher or art paper that comes on a roll and make one big graph for the whole class. Use different-colored bars for the estimate and the actual. Put each student's name under the two bars representing their data. (Fig. 3-8.)

3. Discuss with the class why estimating measurements is an important mathematical skill. Have them measure their hands, arms or feet to use as an aid to estimation. For instance, an adult forearm, wrist to elbow, is about 1 foot, and the distance across the knuckles is about 3 inches. Practice estimating the size of various objects in the room. Always measure the object afterwards to check the estimation. Hold group contests to see who has developed the most skill in estimation.

C. Social studies

1. Sir George Cayley studied the flight of birds and the shape of feathers prior to designing his successful glider (Fig. 3-9.) About 300 years earlier, Leonardo da Vinci also studied birds and flight. In his notebooks, we find drawings of devices similar to modern hang gliders, helicopters, and parachutes. Like Cayley, da Vinci was ahead of his time. Students might enjoy reading one of the many books on da Vinci. The recent book *Leonardo da Vinci: Artist, Inventor and Scientist of the Renaissance* is well written and has wonderful illustrations.

2. This is a great place to stop and think about how everyday things such as zippers, tea bags, and Frisbee's came to be invented. Information on these and many other inventions can be found in Steven Caney's *Invention Book*. Also in this book are chapters on how to be an inventor covering things like keeping a notebook, building a prototype, getting a patent, and starting your own business. This book is a "must read" for young inventors. Another interesting book for older students is *Mothers of Invention: From the Bra to the Bomb, Forgotten Women and their Unforgettable Ideas*, by Vare and Ptacek. This book explains even more of those everyday gizmos we can't imagine being without—such as ice cream cones and that ubiquitous white out—were invented.

The first modern airplane-shaped aircraft

3-9
The Cayley glider made of balsa wood.

D. Language arts

1. As a conclusion to the experiment described previously under "Mathematics," have students compare and contrast their results in writing or in small groups with oral discussion:
   - Compare actual models.
   - Were they exactly alike? Look for differences in the construction of the various gliders.
   - Would any differences that you see account for longer or shorter times in the air for the gliders?
   - How did your estimate vary from your actual results? Were you surprised or was the difference expected?

2. Read more about Sir George Cayley in *Before the Wright Brothers* by Don Berliner. This book also has chapters on Otto Lilienthal and the Wright brothers, whom you will meet later in this book, and nine other aviation pioneers.

3. Would you have liked to have been the first person to soar in one of Sir George's gliders? Write an essay explaining why or why not.

4. Here are some ideas for class discussions:
   a. What did Sir George Cayley wonder about as he watched birds flying?
   b. Do you often wonder? Do you have some ideas in your mind that you would like to develop or invent? How can you convince others of the importance of your ideas? Do you think early inventors might have faced these problems?

c. Think about seeds. There are all kinds of seeds. Seeds are the beginning of new growth. Some seeds, when planted in the right place and cared for properly, will grow into great plants, bushes, or trees. Eventually they will produce new seeds, and the cycle starts all over again. Have you ever thought about how similar this process is to the process of discovery and invention? Discuss your thoughts and observations.

The first controlled, manned aircraft

4

Otto Lilienthal's hang glider, 1896

Otto Lilienthal (leel'-yen-tahl) was an early aviation pioneer from Germany. The Wright brothers once said that he was their greatest inspiration. Lilienthal was very interested in birds, and he studied their flight patterns extensively. His early studies were recorded in a book called *Birdflight as the Basis of Aviation* (Fig. 4-1).

He was the first to recognize and explain the scientific principles of why a curved upper surface works better for a wing than a flat surface. Lilienthal was most famous for a series of experiments he did with what we now call a hang glider. His most important contribution was a flying machine that could be controlled. He did this in his hang glider by moving his body in the direction he wanted to turn.

4-1 *Otto Lilienthal's hang glider: First controlled, manned aircraft.*

He built as many as 18 gliders and was noted for testing his own designs. He and his brother, Gustav, had a cone-shaped hill made near the city of Berlin, (Germany), where they conducted their flights. Historians believe that

Lilienthal conducted more than 2,000 flights. Unfortunately, he was killed in one of his flights in the year 1896.

Fast facts

- ❏ Otto Lilienthal was born May 23, 1848, in Germany and died August 10, 1896, in the crash of one of his gliders.
- ❏ He wanted a hill for his experiments that wouldn't limit him in wind direction. He had one built.
- ❏ He tried to make wings that flapped like a bird but decided that humans would not fly that way.
- ❏ Lilienthal's discoveries influenced the Wright brothers.
- ❏ Otto Lilienthal worked closely with his brother, Gustav.
- ❏ The Lilienthal brothers were known for being very careful researchers.
- ❏ He did his own flight testing in over 2,000 flights.
- ❏ Today's hang gliders are based on Lilienthal's machines.
- ❏ Lilienthal was the first person who demonstrated curved wings in an aerodynamics design.
- ❏ The materials he used to build his gliders were natural, such as willow, wands, and waxed cotton.

Project 4

You build it—Otto Lilienthal's hang glider

The Lilienthal hang glider is an easy-to-make model and is made from a foam meat tray. The little man figure, "Otto," represents a hang glider pilot, like Lilienthal. The only problem with this configuration is that Otto gets broken easily. If the model is flown outdoors on the lawn, Otto will last longer. You might try gluing a toothpick to Otto's body to reinforce him for landings. The hot glue gun works great for this. This glider is so cheap and easy to make that you might want to make several so you can experiment with the wings. Have fun!

A. The basic materials

1. A Styrofoam meat tray, approximately 10 inch × 12 inch, provides the basic material for the glider.

2. A penny is used as the weight for the front of the aircraft.

B. Tools

1. Scissors.

2. Hot glue gun.

C. Safety precautions

1. Be very careful when using a hot glue gun. It can burn fingers. Don't touch the hot glue until it has set and is cooled.

2. Always be careful when cutting with scissors.

D. Steps of construction

1. Make a copy of the template page (Fig. 4-2) on a copy machine. This will save the book from damage. Cut out the templates, then trace the glider components onto the meat tray. Marking pens used for overhead projectors work very well for this, or a pencil will also suffice.

2. Carefully cut out all the components from the meat tray.

3. Cut slots in the fin and horizontal stabilizer as shown in the template.

4. The wing is hot-glued to the fuselage body about 1 inch in back of the nose, as shown in (Fig. 4-3). You might want to build several of these models to experiment with the best wing location.

The first controlled, manned aircraft

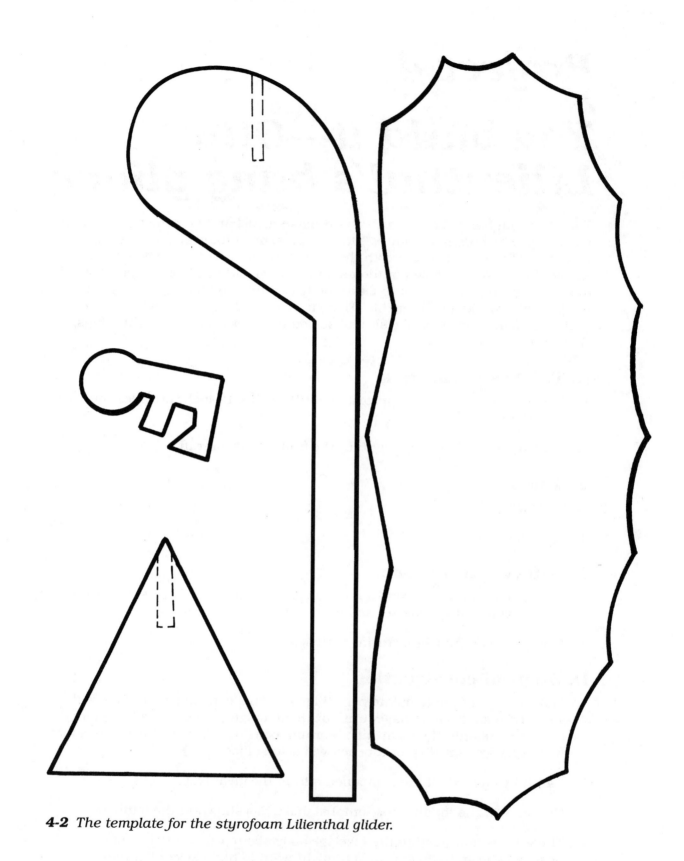

4-2 *The template for the styrofoam Lilienthal glider.*

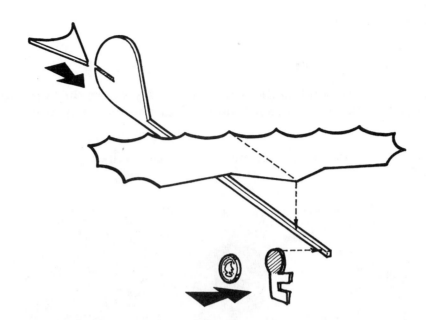

4-3 *The wings are glued to the fuselage. The stabilizer is glued to the fin. Finally, "Otto" is glued to the fuselage and a penny is glued to Otto.*

5. Insert the horizontal stabilizer into the slot in the fin and hot-glue in place.

6. Make sure the horizontal stabilizer and wings are perfectly perpendicular to the fin. Make sure the stabilizer is parallel to the wing.

7. Now hot-glue the penny to the head of "Otto." This will make for better flight characteristics.

8. Carefully hot-glue Otto to the fuselage, as shown in Figs. 4-3 and 4-4.

9. Allow the glue to set up before trying the glider in a flight.

4-4 *The completed glider.*

E. Flying your glider

1. When launching, fly the glider straight away from you. It should make a nice glide back to the floor.

2. You might also try bending the wings up slightly where they are attached at the body. This upsweep is called *dihedral*, and it helps improve stability. (Fig. 4-5.)

3. If it breaks, hey, build another one . . . they're cheap! If it flies, well . . . happy flying.

4-5 *After the glue is set, you might find the Lilienthal glider flies better if you bend the wings slightly upward. This is called "dihedral" and gives the model more stability.*

F. Investigations

1. As you fly the Lilienthal glider, watch the flight path carefully. You will probably notice that it isn't always the same. Sometimes you get a very smooth glide all the way to the ground. Sometimes it glides, stalls, drops, and then lifts again. Sometimes it will even turn and come back toward you. Make up some names for the different types of paths—like smooth, drop, and turn. Try to determine what you do that produces each type.

2. Practice with a friend or parent, then have a friendly competition to see who can produce the greatest distance between launch and landing and who can keep the glider in the air the longest time.

Also recommended

More project ideas!

1. The Windseeker (Fig. 4-6). Write: Mr. Zeke Hermann, Windseeker, Sugar Hill Road, Falls Village, CT 06031. The cost is $3.95. This is one of the most fantastic flyers ever made. Even on calm days, it glides and glides and glides. Because of its design, and because it is inexpensive to own, Dr. Ben says, "Sweetest flying hang glider I've ever seen!"

2. For information about the current sport of hang gliding, write the United States Hang Glider Association, P.O. Box 8300, Colorado Springs, CO 80933.

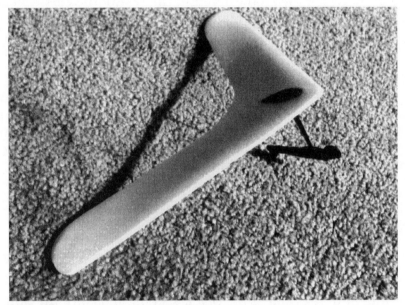

4-6 *The Windseeker after a smooth landing.*

Classroom connections

A. Science

1. Have students carry out the flight path investigation described at the end of the "You build it" section. This is best done as a small group activity with one person acting as the launcher, two students watching the flight path, and two watching the launch very carefully. Have groups report their findings to the class. Discuss with the students the various forces on the glider that produce these paths. Information in the "How they fly" chapter will help you guide the discussion.

B. Mathematics

1. In this activity, students will both estimate and measure the amount of time the Lilienthal glider is aloft. First the students should practice with the gliders until they can achieve a consistent gliding flight. Then each

student should estimate and record the time he or she feels the glider will stay aloft. Students will work in teams of two for the time measurements. Each team will need a stopwatch. (You might want to review stopwatch operation with the students.) While one student is flying a glider, the other team member will measure the time the glider is aloft. After three measurements, the team members reverse jobs. Each student will measure the time his or her glider is aloft three times, then average the three measurements. Have each student record his or her estimate and average time in a chart on the board. Ask the students whose estimates were closest to their averages if they used any special technique to make the estimate. Discuss with the students ways of estimating seconds such as counting "one chimpanzee, two chimpanzees, three chimpanzees." Have them practice counting off 10 seconds. Have someone fly the glider while one student operates the stopwatch and the rest of the class silently counts chimpanzees. See how many students come within one second either way of the actual time. Discuss with the students the difference between this kind of estimate and the "wild guess" sort of estimate that might have been what they did originally.

2. This project can be continued to get some additional practice in making measurements and create an attractive classroom display. Each student will need a 4-foot length of white cotton string. Copy the following instructions for marking the string on the board. (Any colors could be used; the colors of the German flag have been suggested to honor Lilienthal.)

   a. Measure a 3-inch section at the top of the string and tie it into a loop for use as a hook to hang the finished project from the ceiling.

   b. Beginning at the knot of the loop, measure a distance to represent the time of your first flight using the scale 1 inch of string = 1 second of time aloft. With a marker, color this part of the string black.

   c. Beginning at the bottom of the black section, measure the appropriate number of inches for the second flight, and color that section red. Remember the scale!

   d. Beginning at the bottom of the red section, color the last section of the string gold or yellow with a marker, showing the number of seconds the third flight stayed aloft. Cut off all except 2 inches of the remaining string.

   e. Use tape to attach the Lilienthal glider to the end of the string. Experiment with the attachment point until the glider will hang in a level flight position. Write the average of the three flights on the tail of the glider with a marker.

   f. Hang the gliders in the classroom. Ask the students if they observe any patterns relating to the numbers on the tails. (Larger numbers are on the longer strings.) Discuss the fact that the length of the string represents the total of the three times, and the average time is just that total divided by three.

C. Social studies

1. Compile a list of other important inventions of the late 1800s, such as the telephone, the light bulb, the internal combustion engine, and, of course, Coca-Cola. Two good sources of information are *The Picture Book History of Great Inventors*, by Gillian Clements and *Smithsonian Visual Timeline of Inventions*. After a list has been compiled, students should be encouraged to pick one invention and do further research on its development.

D. Language arts

1. Write a paragraph describing the flight patterns of your glider. Use very descriptive language enabling the reader to visualize your description. Did your glider maintain a straight flight path? Did your glider crash? Did Otto break off? Did your glider zoom upward?

2. Write a comparison of the glider with the shortest time aloft and glider with the longest time aloft. Are there obvious visual differences? Were there errors in throwing it? Would you call these pilot errors? What was the takeoff position of each glider? Could you alter the flights of the gliders by attaching more weight to the nose? Less weight?

3. Illustrate the differences between the Cayley glider and the Lilienthal gliders. It has been said that Lilienthal's glider looks like a bat. Describe what a bat looks like. Do you think it looks batlike? Draw batlike features on the wing of your glider if you wish, or color it brightly for display.

4. Middle-school students will enjoy reading about Otto Lilienthal, Sir George Cayley, and others involved in inventing and testing gliders in chapter 3 of *The Wright Brothers: How They Invented the Airplane* by Russell Freedman. This book has very good photographs of some of the early gliders.

The first controlled, manned aircraft

First controlled, powered, & sustained flight

Wilbur & Orville Wright, 1903

Although the Wright brothers achieved their first controlled, sustained, and powered flight on December 17, 1903, they had worked for years first developing gliders. When the brothers were young, their father brought home a flying toy powered by a rubber band. This sparked an interest in flight. Later the boys began experimenting with kites and reading about the works of Otto Lilienthal. Their interest grew as they became adults, and they started building large gliders that were flown like kites. They decided to try to build a human-carrying craft and needed to know where to conduct tests in the most favorable wind conditions. They sent a letter to the U.S. Weather Bureau, and the reply suggested an area by the Atlantic Ocean near Kitty Hawk, North Carolina (Fig. 5-1).

5-1 *The Wright brothers: First controlled, powered, and sustained flight.*

In the late nineteenth century, the brothers had a bicycle shop in Dayton, Ohio. They set up an area of their shop for construction of a glider and then shipped the finished craft, by train, to North Carolina for testing. By 1901, they had a glider that in flight supported the weight of a pilot. This gave the brothers a chance to develop a system for controlling turns.

In experiments conducted in 1902, they incorporated a vertical tail surface that gave them more stable turns. The wings were also warped by a pilot's "hip-saddle." Pitch was controlled by a pilot-operated stick that made a front-mounted "wing" or elevator move up and down. In their Dayton workshop, they also developed a wind "tunnel" for testing the lifting power of various wing shapes.

Since no suitable engine was available to them, the brothers had to build their own—one that would eventually be mounted on their most advanced glider. It had only 12 horsepower, but it did the job.

Finally, on December 14, 1903, a coin was tossed to see who would fly the powered machine. Wilbur won the toss; however, the craft stalled just after takeoff and settled back to the sandy beach with some damage. Three days were required for repairs, and then it was Orville's turn. On the 17th of December, Orville applied the power, and after a ground run of about 40 feet, the "Flyer" rose into the air and flew for 120 feet in a time of 12 seconds. Three more flights were made that day, with the longest being 852 feet in a time of 59 seconds.

Many others attempted powered flight, some with limited success. The main problem was control. This was developed to a high degree by the Wrights during the testing of their gliders. Sustained flight without effective controls would be like driving a powered automobile without a steering wheel. Once the Wrights became masters of controlling their craft, successful flights soon followed. Their scientific minds and methodical testing helped them develop a safe wing and an effective propeller. The Wright Flyer is now on display at the Air & Space Museum, Washington, DC.

Fast facts

❑ Both Wilbur and Orville showed mechanical abilities at an early age.
❑ A skating accident made Wilbur an invalid for several years.
❑ Orville built a printing press and started a weekly newspaper while he was still in high school.
❑ The total cost of their first biplane was $15.00.
❑ In 1908, the Wrights won the first contract ever given for a military airplane.
❑ Wilbur died of typhoid fever on May 30, 1912.
❑ Orville served on the board of the National Advisory Committee for Aeronautics, the forerunner of NASA.
❑ The original Wright Flyer hangs at the entrance of the National Air & Space Museum in Washington, DC.

Project 5

You build it— The Wright Flyer

Let's make a model that looks a lot like the Wright Flyer. We will call it a plane, but it really is a glider since it doesn't have an engine.

A. The basic materials

1. This flying model is also made of Styrofoam meat-tray material. The tray needs to have a flat surface at least 9 inches long. Larger trays will make a larger model. Tan meat trays make a more realistic-looking model.

2. Round toothpicks will make struts that look like the real ones used on the Flyer. For an even more colorful model, use colored toothpicks.

3. A penny can be used for weight on the nose.

B. Tools

1. You will need scissors to cut out the template provided in the text.

2. A hot glue gun, or a white glue like Elmer's, will be needed to bond the wood pieces to the Styrofoam wings.

C. Safety precautions

1. Always be careful when cutting with scissors.

2. Hot glue guns can burn you if you get careless, so don't get in a hurry. Be sure to unplug it when you're through.

D. Steps of construction

1. Make a copy of the template page (Fig. 5-2) on a copy machine. This will save the book from damage. Use the template and trace the parts onto the tray. Be sure to mark the locations of the toothpicks and the boundaries. Then cut out all of the parts using scissors.

2. The template also has the correct size to cut toothpicks for the wings and elevators. After you cut the toothpicks, line them up to be sure they are all the same size, trim any that are too long, and replace ones that are too short.

3. Carefully glue each of the 18 toothpicks into the positions on the lower wing, as shown in Fig. 5-3. Press the toothpicks slightly down into the foam, but not all the way through. If you are using white glue, dip the

First controlled, powered, & sustained flight

47

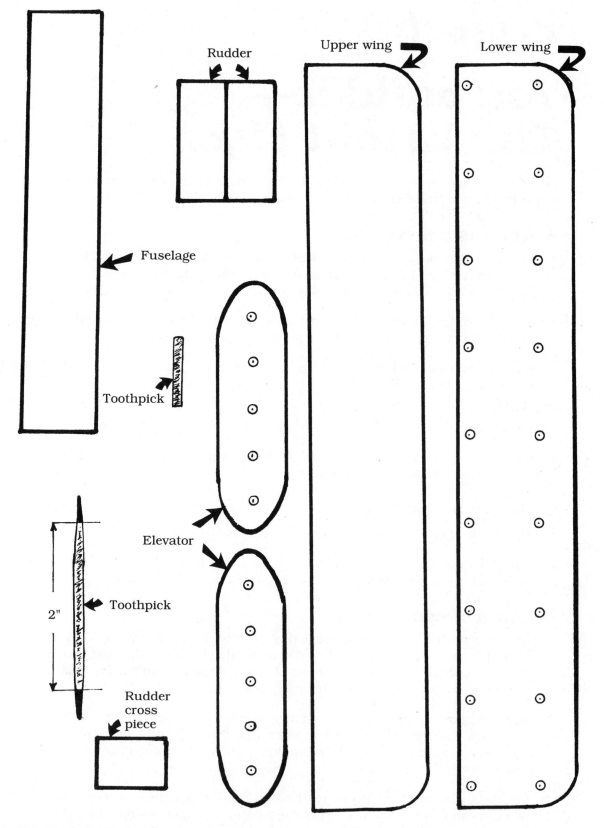

5-2 *Wright Flyer foam glider template.*

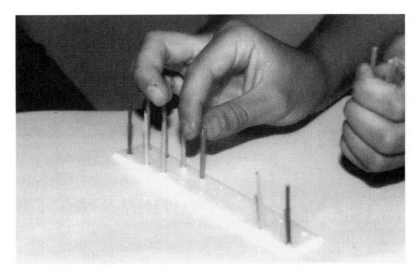

5-3 *Carefully glue each of the 18 toothpicks into the positions on the lower wing.*

toothpick in glue before inserting in the foam. If you are using hot glue, insert the toothpicks in the foam, and then put hot glue around the base of the toothpick. Let the glue dry before proceeding.

4. If you are using white glue, tip the top of each toothpick with glue. Carefully position the upper wing, making sure that all the toothpicks remain vertical. Now press the wings together to get a good bond. It helps to start at one end and work towards the other end, pressing down on each set of toothpicks as you go along. If you are using hot glue, turn the wing over now and drop hot glue around the base of each toothpick, as you did with the bottom wing. Set the wing assembly aside to dry (Fig. 5-4).

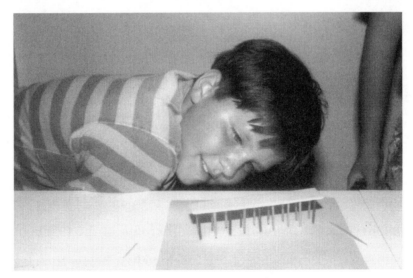

5-4 *Set the wing assembly aside to dry.*

First controlled, powered, & sustained flight

5. For the elevators, cut five toothpicks to the smaller size shown in the template.

6. Dip one end of these toothpicks in glue and mount them carefully on one of the elevator pieces. This piece will be the lower elevator. The toothpicks mount on the dots shown in the template.

7. Then put glue on the other end of each toothpick and carefully mount the upper elevator piece.

8. Set the elevator aside to dry.

9. Cut the two sections of the rudder apart, if you didn't do so initially. Glue the short sides of the rudder crosspiece to a short side of each of the two rudders, making a U. Then set the rudder assembly aside to dry.

10. When all of the parts have dried, you can assemble the plane. Glue the lower side of the wing assembly to the fuselage piece about 2 inches from one end. Study the photograph of the completed model (Fig. 5-5).

5-5 *The completed model.*

11. Glue the open edges of the rudder piece to the fuselage on the short end next to the wing.

12. Mount the elevator into position on the other end of the fuselage (Fig. 5-6).

13. Glue a penny to the underside of the fuselage just below the elevator.

14. If you used white glue, let the model dry for at least an hour.

5-6 *Mount the elevator into position on the other end of the fuselage.*

E. Flying your plane

1. When it's all set up and ready, test fly it, preferably out on the grass or on carpet. You want a soft landing area.

2. If it needs just a little more weight, you might try some modeling clay on the nose.

3. When you get it right . . . . happy flying!

F. Investigations

1. Because we set out to design a plane that would look like the Wright Flyer, it was not possible to make it fly like the Cayley and Lilienthal gliders. Take turns flying your Wright Flyer and one of the other gliders. Notice the differences in the flight characteristics. Compare how they are made and see if you can identify anything that might cause these differences in flight.

Classroom connections

A. Science

1. Use the following problems to introduce or review the concept of average speed (total distance divided by total time). Emphasize that average speed does not tell us how fast the plane was traveling at any particular point in time. Sometimes the plane was traveling faster than the average speed and sometimes slower. Let's say the Wright Flyer had an average speed of 8 feet per second. What this tells us is that if the plane had been moving at a constant speed, it would have traveled 8 feet every second it was in the air. We can use the average speed to find the total distance traveled or total time taken if we know the other one.

The Wright brothers' first successful "Flyer" flew for 120 feet and was in the air for 12 seconds. What was its average speed?

They made several other flights that day. The next one lasted 13 seconds. If the average speed stayed the same, how far did they fly this time?

Again assuming the same average speed, how long would it have taken them to fly 500 feet?

Their last flight on that eventful day was 852 feet in 59 seconds. What was their average speed for this flight?

B. Mathematics

1. Continue the average speed discussion by talking about other cases in which we divide to find out how many of something is in one of something else. Density is another science example. We divide mass by volume to find out how many grams are in 1 cubic centimeter of the object. Examples abound at the grocery store. If I buy 3 pounds of bananas for $1.20, that is $0.40 for 1 pound. Pretend that the class is going to sell candy bars to raise money for a field trip. In order to have enough money, the class needs to sell 500 candy bars. How many candy bars does each (or one) student have to sell? Your students will be coming up with examples for days.

2. Now that you have the students thinking about division as "for one" or "for every," challenge them to come up with an example for which that is not the reason we divide. After concentrating on the "for one" meaning, they will probably have to stop and think awhile. Any of the previous examples can be turned around. If bananas cost $0.40 for 1 pound, how many pounds can I buy for $1.20? Now we are asking how many times will $0.40 fit into $1.20, which is a very different question and illustrates a different meaning for division.

C. Social studies

1. Use a U.S. map to chart your route from Dayton, Ohio to Kitty Hawk, North Carolina—as if you were traveling there today. List the interstate highways, the regular highways, and causeways along your route. Name the states through which you would drive. Use the scale of miles on the map to figure how many miles you would travel on your route. Compare the distance traveled on your route to routes other students have chosen. Is the route that is the shortest in distance always shortest in time? Why or why not?

2. Using the Wright Flyer as a model, each student should draw and cut out a small biplane and label his or her name and the city where he or she was born. Attach a length of cotton string to each of these biplanes. On a large wall map, use thumbtacks to attach the planes to the periphery of the map and the other end of the string to the cities where students were born. Using atlases or folding maps, have students calculate how far it would be

to travel on roads from their birthplaces to their school. If students are native to the area, they might calculate the distance to the home of a grandparent, parent, or friend. After this calculation has been made, have students measure "as the crow flies," and calculate the difference to see how much faster flight makes travel.

3. Create a timeline of the history of flight, beginning with the Wright brothers and going forward to the present day. Two good books to use to gather your data are *Flight: Fliers and Flying Machines* from the Franklin Watts Timelines series and *The Timeline of Discovery and Invention* by Peter North and Philip Wilkinson. Compare your timeline with another student's. Did you choose the same events to include? If not, why do you think you might have chosen differently?

D. Language arts

1. Read one of the many books that have been written about the Wright brothers. I particularly like these two: for elementary students, *The Story of the Flight At Kitty Hawk* by Conrad Stein and, for older students, *The Wright Brothers: How They Invented the Airplane* by Russell Freedman.

2. Wilbur Wright once said the following: "From the time we were little children, my brother Orville and myself lived together, played together, worked together, and in fact, thought together. We usually owned all of our toys in common, talked over our thoughts and aspirations so that nearly everything that was done in our lives has been the result of conversations, suggestions, and discussions between us." Choose one of these related themes to write about:
   a. Do you have a brother or sister? If not, do you have a close friend or cousin? Do you share your thoughts and feelings, and your toys with this person?
   b. Consider your parents. Do they have a very close relationship with one of their brothers or sisters? Were they always close to each other like the Wright brothers were, or did they develop a closer relationship as they became older?
   c. Do you think the success the Wright brothers had was directly related to their closeness? What if they had not been so willing to share? Would their lives have been changed?

3. Here are some additional ideas for essays or class discussions:
   a. The Montgolfier brothers invented the hot-air balloon, but they were not the first to fly in it. Describe how you think the Wright brothers must have felt after they worked several years developing their flying machine and then they were able to fly in it. Describe the emotions you think they might have experienced. Do you think their success made them more confident. Would you feel more confident if your model was the best "flyer" in class?
   b. Have you ever had an idea that you wanted to make come true—and were actually able to see it happen? Describe what it was.

c. A barnstormer was the name given to an adventure-seeking pilot. This person actually crawled out on the wings and performed tricks to entertain people who were watching from below. Think of some adventure-seeking occupations people have today that might be as thrilling as being a barnstormer. Compare and contrast the dangers and thrills of barnstorming and some modern-day occupations.

First American woman to get a pilot's license & fly the English Channel

6

Harriet Quimby, 1911

Harriet Quimby was born on May 1, 1884, in California. Her parents were from New England. She grew up and was educated in both France and the United States. Harriet was fortunate enough to be tutored privately. Many young women of that time were not allowed to go to school because people believed that only men needed an education (Fig. 6-1).

6-1 *Harriet Quimby: First American woman to get a pilot's license and to fly the English Channel.*

Harriet Quimby was intelligent and had a keen sense of humor. She left San Francisco and moved to New York City in hopes of becoming a journalist. She became interested in airplanes and automobiles, and she rode with one driver who reached 100 miles per hour. She loved it.

She entered the Moissant School for pilots, where she and two other women took training to become flyers. They had a friendly competition to see who would be the first to get her license. Harriet won by successfully passing the three tests necessary to qualify, and she was awarded her license on August 11, 1911, becoming the first American woman to achieve that certificate. The first flying test included five alternate right and left turns around pylons, the second test included flying figure eights, and the final test covered accurate landings.

Miss Quimby traveled for a few years, performing in air shows with other pilots. Eventually she decided to try to become the first woman to fly the English Channel. She achieved that goal and was later awarded the land around the spot where she landed her airplane.

On July 1, 1912, Harriet flew her plane at an aviation meet near Boston, Massachusetts. As she flew over the crowd, her controls malfunctioned and the airplane went upside down. Both she and her passenger fell out because they were not wearing seat belts. Both died as they plunged into Dorchester Bay.

Unfortunately, Harriet was the first woman to be killed in an airplane-related accident. This resulted in pilots everywhere taking a more serious look at the importance of seat-belt safety. Her death eventually saved lives as a result of seat-belt awareness.

Fast facts

❏ Miss Quimby received the first American pilot's license to be given to a woman.

❏ Harriet Quimby was the first woman to fly across the English Channel.

❏ There were no fancy instruments on these early planes. The English Channel flight was the first time she had even used a compass for navigation.

❏ She loved to write and was a writer before becoming a pilot.

❏ She flew planes at state and county fairs in many parts of America as entertainment for the crowds.

❏ She also flew in a flying demonstration at the inauguration of a president of Mexico.

❏ She was well respected by other pilots, men and women alike.

Project 6

You build it—Harriet Quimby's Bleriot

Harriet Quimby's Bleriot was a beautiful little aircraft, and even for an advanced model builder, it would be difficult to construct one that would look and fly right. The author tested scores of models to find just the right one for this unit. And . . . this is it! Consider purchasing this model, made by Estes, the acclaimed manufacturer of Estes Rockets. It is called the "Hi Lite Light Glider." If you use your imagination, you can see that it resembles Harriet Quimby's airplane. It has a tiny fuselage, big wings, big tail, tiny wheels, and a fat propeller just like the Bleriot. Estes has designed it to fly, and fly it does. You will love building and flying this model—and it's inexpensive.

A. The basic materials

1. The Estes Light Glider Kit (Fig. 6-2) can be purchased at many toy stores. If you can't find it locally, you can request a catalog from Estes, 1295 H Street, Penrose, CO 81240.

2. White or hot glue to bond the tail mount to the fuselage is helpful, but not required.

6-2 *The Estes Hi-Lite model airplane kit. This is our "Bleriot." Like Harriet Quimby's airplane, this one has big wings, a tiny fuselage, little wheels, and a big fat propeller. She loved to fly, and you too will love to fly your model!*

B. Tools

None.

C. Safety precautions

1. When the plane is prepared for flight, a rubber band is wound up and has stored energy ready to make the propeller turn. A sharp propeller can hurt people if this model is thrown at them. The propeller can also hurt your

First American woman to get a pilot's license & fly the English Channel

57

hand if released unexpectedly during winding. Make every effort to fly your aircraft in an open, safe area away from trees, small children, and pets.

D. Steps of construction

1. Estes has kindly granted permission to reprint their instructions in this book (Fig. 6-3). Look them over, and you'll see just how easy it is to build this model. Once familiar with the instructions, go for it!

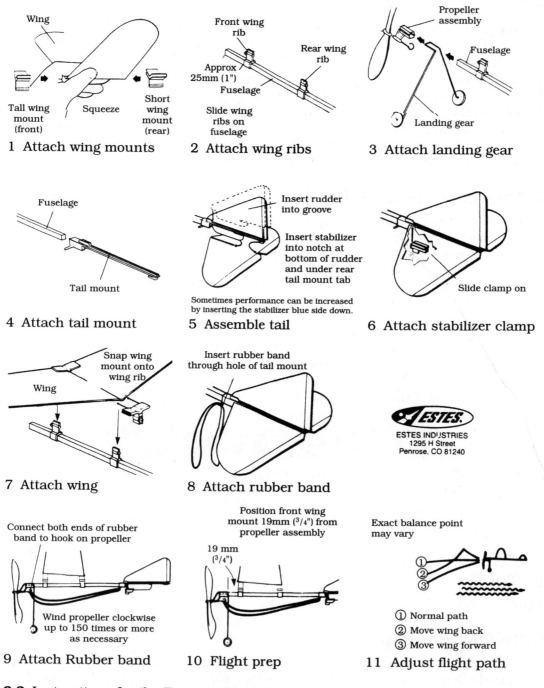

6-3 *Instructions for the Estes Light Glider Kit.*

Chapter 6

LIGHT GLIDER™

Hi Lite™   EST 4000

Parts list

1	Front wing rib
2	Tall wing mount
3	Rear wing rib
4	Short wing mount
5	Stabilizer clamp
6	Fuselage
7	Landing gear
8	Propeller
9	Rubber band
10	Wing
11	Rudder
11	Stabilizer
13	Tail mount

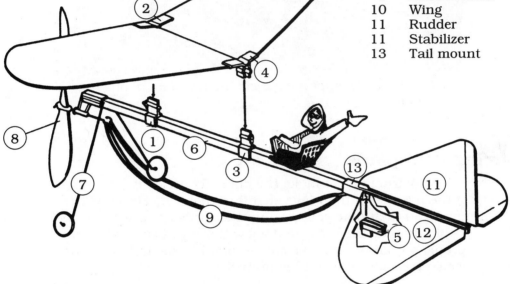

6-4 *Know your parts!*

2. Become familiar with the parts, as shown in Fig. 6-4.

3. Attach wing mounts first.

4. Attach wing ribs next as shown.

5. Insert the landing gear and fuselage into the propeller assembly.

6. Attach the tail mount. (We found that gluing the tail mount to the fuselage helped keep it from coming apart during landing.)

7. Assemble the tail.

8. Attach the stabilizer clamp.

First American woman to get a pilot's license & fly the English Channel

9. Attach the wing. (Hey, it's beginning to look like the Bleriot, huh?)

10. Attach the rubber band provided in the kit.

11. Position the front wing mount about ¾ inches in back of the propeller assembly (Fig. 6-5).

6-5 *Dave and Jennifer have their "Bleriot" just about ready to fly.*

E. Flying your plane

1. Follow Estes' instructions to make the plane fly perfectly. You might need to adjust the position of the wings slightly to achieve a level flight. Counting to 150 each time you wind up the rubber band can be tedious, but you will find that after counting a few times you can tell when it is wound properly from the way the rubber band looks and how much resistance you feel as you wind the propeller.

2. Now imagine Harriet Quimby sitting in the cockpit just taking off on her epic flight over the English Channel. When you let it go, she flies! . . . Happy flying, Harriet! (Fig. 6-6.)

F. Investigations

1. Practice with your airplane until you can get consistently good flights. Now wind the rubber band more than you have been. Does the plane fly a greater distance? Try winding the rubber band less than you have been. Does the plane still fly? Can you explain your results?

2. Mark the location of the wings that produces your best flights. Move the wings ½ inch forward and fly the plane. How is the flight different? Move the wings ½ inch behind the position you marked. Is this flight different from your previous one? Read the "Science" section of "Classroom connections" for some ideas on what causes these changes.

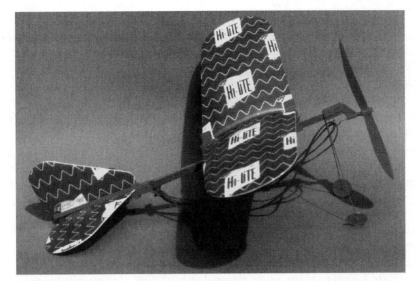

6-6 *The Hi-Lite model by Estes, a great little flyer.*

Also recommended

More project ideas!

1. *AVIATION AND LIGHT GLIDERS.* Write: Mr. James H. Kranich, Estes Industries, 1295 H Street, Penrose, Colorado 81240 and inquire about this and other publications offered. This book was designed as a curriculum guide by James H. Kranich, Educational Manager of Estes Industries. It specifically uses the ultralight gliders offered by the company as a guide to better understanding airplanes. Chapters include: Myths; Balloon History; Glider History; Airplane History; Bernoulli's Principle; The Wing; Connect the Dots; Control Surface Effects; Aerodynamics; Climbs and Dives; Coordinated Turn; The Cockpit; Flight Controls; a Maneuver Puzzle; Airport Diagrams; Communication Codes; and a Crossword Puzzle Review. This book is an excellent offering for students, parents, and teachers. It would make a wonderful gift for a youngster.

2. Academy of Model Aeronautics. To obtain information about model airplane building and flying, get in touch with: A.M.A. 1810 Samuel Morse Drive, Reston, VA 22090.

Classroom connections

A. Science

1. After students have practiced with their planes for a while, ask them to investigate how the position of the wings changes the flight path. Ask someone to describe to the class what happens if the wings are too far forward. Ask someone else to describe what happens if the wings are too far back. Explain how these paths are produced as a result of the relative positions of the center of gravity and center of lift. We think of the weight of an object as being a single force, but actually it is the sum of millions of

First American woman to get a pilot's license & fly the English Channel

tiny forces—the gravitational attraction of the Earth on each atom. Luckily we do not really have to worry about this because every object behaves as if its weight were a single force acting at a point we call the center of gravity of the object. Airplanes also have a point called the center of lift, at which we can imagine the lift force acting even though it is actually distributed over the entire wing surface. To understand the flight patterns that have been observed, it is helpful to think of the airplane as a lever with the fulcrum at the center of gravity. If the center of lift is in front of the fulcrum, the lift pushes the nose of the airplane up, and it rises into a stall. If the center of lift is behind the fulcrum, the lift pushes the tail up and the plane dives. As you move the wing, you are adjusting the center of lift to be at or just slightly in front of the fulcrum, which produces a stable, level flight.

2. Ask students to wind up the rubber bands in their airplanes while holding the fuselage beneath the wing. Then, without moving the hand holding the plane, release the propeller. Students will feel a strong wind blowing against their hands. Now have them look at the shape of the propeller. As it turns counterclockwise, the leading edge is further forward than the trailing edge. This throws air toward the back of the plane. Since the propeller is exerting a force on the air toward the rear, Newton's Third Law tells us that the air must be exerting a forward force on the propeller, which pushes the plane forward.

B. Mathematics

1. Since proper balance is so important to this plane and other gliders, let's do an activity on balance that incorporates lots of mathematical ideas also. Each group of students will need a ruler, a 35-mm film canister (or any cylindrical object), some paper clips, and some modeling clay. You might want to prepare a set of instructions similar to the following for each group.

To get ready, place the canister on its side on top of the clay and push down firmly so that it is held in a stable position.

Now balance the ruler horizontally on the canister. Write down the position on the ruler, that is in the center of the canister. It should be around 6 inches. Make a mark on the canister showing this position also.

Now we want to try balancing different numbers of paper clips on the ruler. Start with something easy. Place one paper clip 4 inches from the center position that you wrote down. Figure out where you need to place a second clip to make it balance.

Next put three paper clips 1 inch from the center position. Where could you put one paper clip on the other side to make it balance?

Is there somewhere you could put two paper clips on that side to make it balance?

Keep trying varying combinations until you are sure you have figured out the pattern.

To test yourself, put two paper clips 5 inches from the center position. How many ways can you figure out to balance the system? Is there a way to do it without putting all your paper clips at the same place? Check all your solutions to see if they work.

By experimenting, students should figure out that in order to balance, the number of paper clips on one side multiplied by their distance from the center should equal the same quantity for the other side. For instance, the last example of two paper clips 5 inches from the center can be solved by putting the same thing on the other side or by putting five clips 2 inches from the center or by putting three clips 3 inches from the center and one clip 1 inch from the center ($3 \times 3 + 1 \times 1 = 2 \times 5$). There are many other ways as long as the total adds up to 10. If students are restricted to only using one location on each side of the ruler, either proportions or ratios can be emphasized in examining the pattern.

C. Social studies

1. Eleven years after Harriet Quimby received her license, Bessie Coleman became the first black woman to earn a pilot's license. As a young girl growing up in Texas, Bessie developed a love of books. Her mother, a former slave, always encouraged her to "become somebody." She dreamed of going to college but had to drop out after one semester due to financial difficulties. Eventually she moved to Chicago and became a beautician. During World War I, Bessie watched newsreels of fighter planes and began to dream of flying. Unfortunately, few flight schools would accept female students, and none would accept a black woman. She refused to let go of her dream. After being advised to go to France where attitudes toward women and people of color were more liberal, she went to night school to learn French. Meanwhile she worked to save enough money for the trip to Europe. Eventually, she did study flying in France and earned her pilot's license there. She dreamed of opening a flight school to train black pilots and began giving exhibitions to raise money. Like Harriet Quimby and many other early pilots, she was killed in a flying accident at an early age. Elementary students can read more about Bessie Coleman in *Flying Free: America's First Black Aviators* by Philip Hart. Older students will enjoy *Queen Bess: Daredevil Aviator* by Doris Rich.

2. If you read about modern airplane crashes, sometimes people refer to the "black box." This is a recording device that is found in most larger airplanes to record what happens in flight. If the plane crashes, this "Data flight recorder" can offer valuable information to the investigators concerning the cause of the crash. See what you can learn about the Data Flight Recorder. You might like to interview a pilot or visit a local airport to complete your report. Also, in the "Resources" chapter at the end of this book is the address of the Federal Aviation Administration. You might want to write them a letter and ask them for information about the data flight recorder.

D. Language arts

1. Junior-high students will enjoy reading about Harriet Quimby in one of the following books: *Ladybirds: The Untold Story of Women Pilots in America* by Henry Holden, *Sky Stars: The History of Women in Aviation* by Ann Hodgman and Rudy Djabbaroff, or *Women with Wings: Female Flyers in Fact and Fiction* by Mary Cadogan.

2. Harriet Quimby loved adventure. She was constantly seeking excitement in her life. Write a paragraph discussing activities that you consider to be adventurous. Is adventure always thrilling? Is it always dangerous? Is it necessary to continue making wise choices when seeking interesting things to do? Discuss your paragraph with a partner, your parents, or members of your class.

3. Write a short poem about aviators. They were a very brave group of people. Some words that you might want to use are: rudder, aileron, flaps, wing, propeller, throttle, cockpit, takeoff, flight . . .

4. Pearl S. Buck was a missionary and author who won the Nobel Prize for literature in 1938. She spent most of her life in China, and she once said, "All things are possible until they are proved impossible—and even the impossible might only be so, as of now." Choose one of these related projects to pursue:

   a. Choose a friend, grandparent, or nursing home resident to interview. Talk with them about different events that have happened during their lifetimes which were considered impossible when they were young. Some of these might be automobiles, airplanes, television, rockets, satellites . . .

   b. You might be considering a problem in your own life that seems "impossible" right now. Sometimes talking to other people helps. Talk to a parent, teacher, counselor, or concerned friend who might help you with the "impossible" problem.

   c. Brainstorm a list of problems in your school. Choose one of them and brainstorm a list of solutions with your classmates. Set an appointment with your principal to discuss the topic. Hopefully, one of your solutions to this "impossible" problem will meet with success.

He made aviation believable

Charles A. Lindbergh, 1927

7

Charles A. Lindbergh was not the first person to cross the great Atlantic Ocean, but he was the first to fly it alone. A prize in the amount of $25,000 was offered to the first person who could fly nonstop from New York to Paris. The historical flight was made on May 20–21, 1927, by Lindbergh in an aircraft called the "Spirit of St. Louis." A group of St. Louis businesspeople sponsored the construction of the Ryan-built airplane, and that's where it got its name (Fig. 7-1).

Lindbergh, or "Lucky Lindy," as the media called him, was a native of Minnesota, and he learned to fly in Lincoln, Nebraska. He started his career by flying from town to town offering rides and putting on aerial shows. This activity was known as "barnstorming." Later he joined the U.S. Army Signal Corps as a reserve pilot. He also flew mail between Chicago and St. Louis.

His 3,614-mile flight from New York to Paris lifted off from Roosevelt Air Field, at 7.54 a.m. on the 20th of May, 1927. He flew through storms, fog, and icy conditions before landing at Le Bourget

7-1 *Charles A. Lindbergh: He made aviation believable—The Spirit of St. Louis.*

Airport in Paris. His greatest challenge was not the weather conditions, but staying awake.

After 28 hours, the coast of Ireland appeared. He flew on, and as daylight faded, he eventually saw Paris. Paris is known as the "City of Light," and the headlamps of hundreds of cars going to the airport to greet the aviator guided him to his destination. Once he landed, the crowd went wild with enthusiasm. He was a hero admired around the world.

More than any other flight in history, Lindbergh's success proved to people that aircraft were safe. Everyone realized that it was possible to make long flights, even over great oceans. People recognized that air travel would soon take them to places all over the world. He brought credibility to aviation. His Spirit of St. Louis now hangs in permanent display at the National Air and Space Museum in Washington, DC.

Fast facts

❏ Lindbergh was born February 4, 1902, in Detroit Michigan. He died August 26, 1974, on Maui Island in Hawaii.

❏ He spent his childhood in Little Falls, Minnesota.

❏ Lindbergh's father was a U.S. congressman from 1907 to 1917.

❏ Charles Lindbergh married Anne Spencer Morrow, who later served as his navigator and copilot, in 1929. Both he and his wife were accomplished authors.

❏ He won a Pulitzer Prize in 1954.

❏ He experimented with Alexis Carrel, a French surgeon, to develop an artificial heart pump.

Project 7

You build it—Stand-up historical flight

Lindbergh's flight was one of the greatest single accomplishments in aviation history. More than any other flight, it convinced everyone that safe, speedy world travel was possible. Lindbergh's flight has been compared to the Apollo 11 flight, in which man landed on the moon. Like Lindbergh's flight, it wasn't necessarily the craft that was so incredible. It was the feat itself and the enormous distances traveled. The flight to the moon proved to people that spaceflight was possible. In 1927, flying solo across the Atlantic Ocean was just as incredible.

Instead of making another flying project for this chapter, we have created a piece of stand-up art to help you remember the importance of accomplishment.

A. The basic materials

1. A file folder or construction paper or similar heavy paper.

2. Marking pen.

3. White glue or rubber cement.

B. Tools

1. Scissors.

C. Safety precautions

1. Always be careful when cutting with scissors.

D. Steps of construction

1. Make a copy of the Spirit of St. Louis (Fig. 7-2) and the "map" of Lindbergh's flight from New York to Paris, France (Fig. 7-3). This will save the book from damage. Enlarge the airplane by 200%.

7-2 *The Spirit of St. Louis.*

2. Cut out both the plane and the map.

3. Using rubber cement or white glue, bond the airplane to a file folder or construction paper. Cut around the outline of the plane.

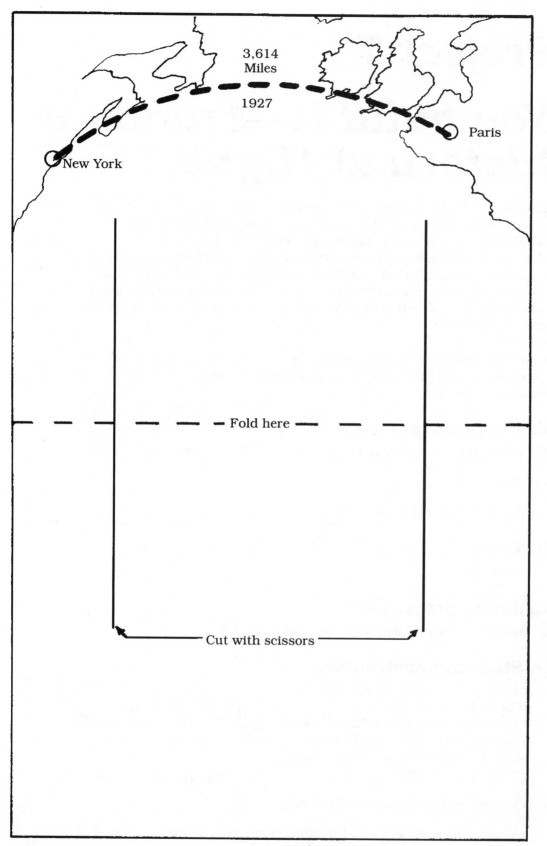

7-3 *Lindbergh's flight from New York to Paris.*

4. Using rubber cement or white glue, bond the flight "map" to the other piece of file folder or construction paper.

5. Make two cuts in the "map" on the solid lines.

6. Fold the edges down, and fold the center cut section up to make a stand for the airplane.

7. Glue the airplane on the front section of the stand so that it is nicely displayed with the map in the background (Fig. 7-4).

8. Study the airplane and the map. Say to yourself, "Way to go Lucky Lindbergh. Good job!"

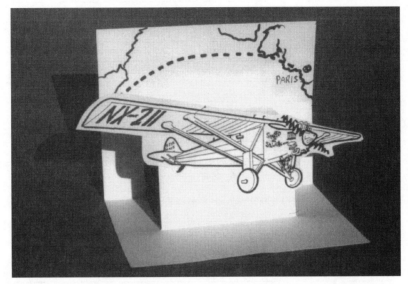

7-4 *Your stand-up Spirit of St. Louis and the map of its flight from New York to Paris.*

Classroom connections

A. Science

1. Since we don't have a model with which to perform experiments in this chapter, let's do some reading. Elementary students should learn a lot from *Eureka! It's an Airplane!* by Jeanne Bendick. This book teaches many science concepts related to flying using the theme of how one might invent something to solve a series of problems.

2. Staying awake was a major problem for Lindbergh. Look up some information on the studies that have been done on sleep deprivation. You will find that our bodies can react very strangely to lack of sleep.

B. Mathematics

1. Using the activity log provided at the end of this chapter, document each hour of your time for a period of 33.5 hours. That is the length of time it took Lindbergh to fly across the Atlantic and land in Paris, France.

He made aviation believable

Table 7-1 Activity Log.

From	To	Activity
8:00 AM	9:00 AM	
9:00 AM	10:00 AM	
10:00 AM	11:00 AM	
11:00 AM	12:00 PM	
12:00 PM	1:00 PM	
1:00 PM	2:00 PM	
2:00 PM	3:00 PM	
3:00 PM	4:00 PM	
4:00 PM	5:00 PM	
5:00 PM	6:00 PM	
6:00 PM	7:00 PM	
7:00 PM	8:00 PM	
8:00 PM	9:00 PM	
9:00 PM	10:00 PM	
10:00 PM	11:00 PM	
11:00 PM	12:00 AM	
12:00 AM	1:00 AM	
1:00 AM	2:00 AM	
2:00 AM	3:00 AM	
3:00 AM	4:00 AM	
4:00 AM	5:00 AM	
5:00 AM	6:00 AM	
6:00 AM	7:00 AM	
7:00 AM	9:00 AM	
8:00 AM	9:00 AM	
9:00 AM	10:00 AM	
10:00 AM	11:00 AM	
11:00 AM	12:00 PM	
12:00 PM	1:00 PM	
1:00 PM	2:00 PM	
2:00 PM	3:00 PM	
3:00 PM	4:00 PM	
4:00 PM	5:00 PM	
5:00 PM	6:00 PM	
6:00 PM	6:30 PM	

Compare your chart with that of a classmate. How is it similar? How is it different? Discuss your conclusions with other classmates and your teacher. Classify the different activities into groups, such as eating, school work, play, video games, etc. Make a graph depicting how long you spend on specific activities. You could make a bar graph or a circle graph. Now add up how much time each individual spends in each category of activity to make a class graph. Display your findings in the hallway for others to observe.

C. Social sciences

1. On the world map in your classroom, mark the flight Charles Lindbergh took from New York to Paris. Why do you think he chose the route that he did? Reread the biography at the beginning of this chapter and look for clues. Using the scale on the world map, measure a piece of string to represent the distance Lindbergh flew from New York to Paris (3,614 miles). Place the string between New York and Paris and decide if he used the shortest possible route. Use a piece of string to measure the straight-line distance between New York and Paris. Don't forget to use the map scale to convert the length of the string into the number of miles it represents. Now do the same thing on a globe. You probably won't get the same answer. Globes are the only way to portray distances accurately. All flat maps distort distances and positions. Depending on how the flat map is made, different parts of the Earth are more distorted. Look up the meaning of "great circle distance."

2. Construct a timeline illustrating the major events of Charles Lindbergh's life. Several books you could consult for information about Lindbergh are listed in the "Language arts" section.

3. There were many heroes of flight in this era, with new records being set every year. The stories of women pilots are particularly interesting because not only did they have to survive the dangers inherent in the flight itself, but they also had to overcome the prejudices against women pilots that were common at that time. Upon hearing of Lindbergh's flight Ruth Elder became determined to become "Lady Lindy," the first woman to fly across the Atlantic. She made her attempt in October, 1927, and almost made it successfully. An oil leak forced her down not far from her goal, and she gained the dubious distinction being the first woman ever rescued on a transatlantic flight. In 1930, Amy Johnson became the first woman to fly solo from England to Australia, a trip that took 20 days. In 1935, Jean Batten set a new speed record for the crossing of the southern Atlantic Ocean and went on to set many other records. Younger students will enjoy reading about Johnson and Batten in *Women of the Air* by David Mondey. *Ladybirds: The Untold Story of Women Pilots in America* by Holden and Griffith, and *Sky Stars: The History of Women in Aviation* by Hodgman and Djabbaroff are more appropriate for older students.

4. The importance of Lindbergh's flight in the history of modern civilization has been emphasized in this chapter. Brainstorm some other events or inventions that had major impacts on the history of the world. Assign groups to prepare a report on different items from your brainstormed list.

He made aviation believable

The report should include a description of the event or invention, what effect it has had, and what might have been different if it had not happened. Students might enjoy reading *53½ Things that Changed the World and Some that Didn't!* by West and Parker.

D. Language arts

1. Read one of the many books that have been written about the Lindberghs. I particularly like these: for elementary students, *Lindbergh* by Chris Demarest or *The Story of The Spirit of St. Louis* by Conrad Stein; and, for older students, *Lindbergh Alone* by Brendan Gill.

2. Read *Flight* by Robert Burleigh aloud to the class. This book for younger readers describes Lindbergh's flight in detail. It is beautifully written and reads more like poetry than prose. Read aloud, it will bring the flight to life for both children and adults.

3. Using the personal time journal made in the math activity, write your impression of how long 33.5 hours seemed to you. Would it be difficult for you to stay awake that long? Could you sit in one position for such a long time? What would you think about trying to keep your mind alert? Would you be willing to make such a personal sacrifice for something you really believed in?

4. Imagine that you are alone in the cockpit of the "Spirit of St. Louis." You haven't spoken to anyone in hours, and suddenly an insect begins flying around inside the cockpit with you. Would it be a distraction, or would you welcome the company? Would you wonder where the insect came from? Write a story about your hours alone in this situation.

5. Will Rogers, a well-known humorist in the early part of this century, once said, "In order to succeed, you must know what you are doing, like what you are doing, and believe in what you are doing." Here are some related questions to ponder and discuss with a parent, friend, or class group.
   a. Do you think Charles Lindbergh liked what he did? Discuss why you think he did or did not.
   b. When you succeed at something, how do you feel? It might be a school project, sports, or a hobby. Does your success make you want to try harder?
   c. Do you need to believe in yourself to find success? Does it help to have the support of your family and friends when you are trying to achieve a goal?
   d. Which of the three ideals in Will Roger's quote is the most important: knowing, believing, or liking? Why do you think this is true? Think of a personal experience related to one of these ideals.

First to exceed the speed of sound

8

Chuck Yeager's X-1, 1947

Charles Elwood Yeager, better known as Chuck Yeager, was born on February 13, 1923. He was the second of five children. He grew up in West Virginia. His father was an excellent mechanic, and Chuck always felt that he had inherited his father's "knack with machines." He received his best grades in school in mathematics and typing and anything else that required mechanical dexterity (Fig. 8-1).

Yeager first joined the Army in 1941 to fight in World War II. He was commissioned an officer and later entered training to become an Army Air Corps fighter pilot. During the war, Yeager became an "ace" by shooting down five enemy aircraft.

After the war was over, he returned to the United States, where he helped train pilots and later became a test pilot. It was in this job that he ended up at Muroc Dry Lake, where rocket aircraft testing was being conducted. Chuck was

8-1 *Chuck Yeager, first to exceed the speed of sound—The X-1.*

eventually given the opportunity to fly the Bell XS-1, an aircraft designed to go through the "sound barrier." The speed of sound is 760 miles per hour at sea level, and it decreases as you go higher. At a speed of 662 miles per hour at an altitude of more than 40,000 feet, the XS-1, later called the "X-1," broke the record, and Yeager became the fastest man alive. He retired from the Air Force in 1975 as a Brigadier General.

Fast facts

❏ In 1947, Charles Yeager was the first person to break the sound barrier.

❏ The day before he was to fly, Yeager fell from a horse and broke several ribs. He did not want to lose his chance to fly the X-1, so he flew in great pain without telling anyone except his wife, Glennis, and a friend, Jack Ridley.

❏ The X-1 burned 13,000 pounds of fuel in 2½ minutes.

❏ Breaking the sound barrier was not made public for eight months because it was considered important to "national security."

❏ He was given the Presidential Medal of Freedom by President Ronald Reagan.

Project 8

You build it—
Chuck Yeager's X-1

A. The basic materials

1. Foam pipe insulation 12 inches long and 2 inches in diameter will be needed for the fuselage (Fig. 8-2).

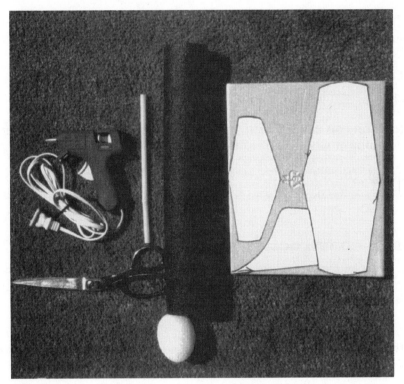

8-2 For Chuck Yeager's X-1, you will need foam tubing, a meat tray, scissors, a styrofoam egg, and a hot glue gun.

2. The nose cone will be made from a Styrofoam "egg." This foam egg can be found at craft stores nationwide. The egg should be about 2 inches in diameter and 2 inches long.

3. Meat trays from supermarkets make perfect "wings" and tail surfaces. You will need one that gives you about 9¼ inches × 7½ inches of working area. This is the "working bottom" of the tray. Or you could use several smaller ones.

4. A flat stick, like a stirring stick from a paint store.

First to exceed the speed of sound

5. A piece of medium to fine sandpaper.

6. You'll need a piece of string or fishing line about 15 feet long.

7. A toy balloon will power your rocket. (Long, tube-shaped balloons work a little better than round ones.)

8. Masking tape.

The Competition Orange spray paint used for Chuck Yeager's X-1 Project was Testor's Spray Enamel #1628 Gloss Orange. It was purchased at a local hobby shop for $2.12.

B. Tools

1. Large scissors will be needed to cut the foam trays.

2. A hot glue gun is a must to make the foam tray material stick to the foam pipe insulation.

C. Safety precautions

1. Always be careful when cutting with scissors.

2. Hot glue guns can burn you if you get careless, so don't get in a hurry. Be sure to unplug it when you're through.

3. Even though the X-1 has a soft foam nose, it can still hurt someone if thrown or projected. Fly it in open areas away from small children and pets.

D. Steps of construction

1. Make a copy of the template page on a copy machine. This will save the book from damage. Using the template provided, cut out the wings, fin, and stabilizer (Fig. 8-3).

2. Put the templates down on the "working bottom" of the foam meat tray and either trace the wings, fin, and stabilizer outlines, or rubber cement them to the tray (Fig. 8-4).

3. Using large scissors, cut out the wing, fin, and stabilizer.

4. Now cut the wing in the center (at the widest point, from front to rear.)

5. Do the same with the stabilizer. Cut it into two equal parts.

6. Glue a piece of sandpaper approximately 4 inches long to a flat stick, like a stirring stick from a paint store (Fig. 8-5). Using this sanding stick, sand the edges of the wings, stabilizers, and fin where they will bond to the main body. You need to create a nice flat edge.

7. Using the blowup diagram as a guide, hot-glue the fin to the fuselage. Make sure it stands up straight (Fig. 8-6).

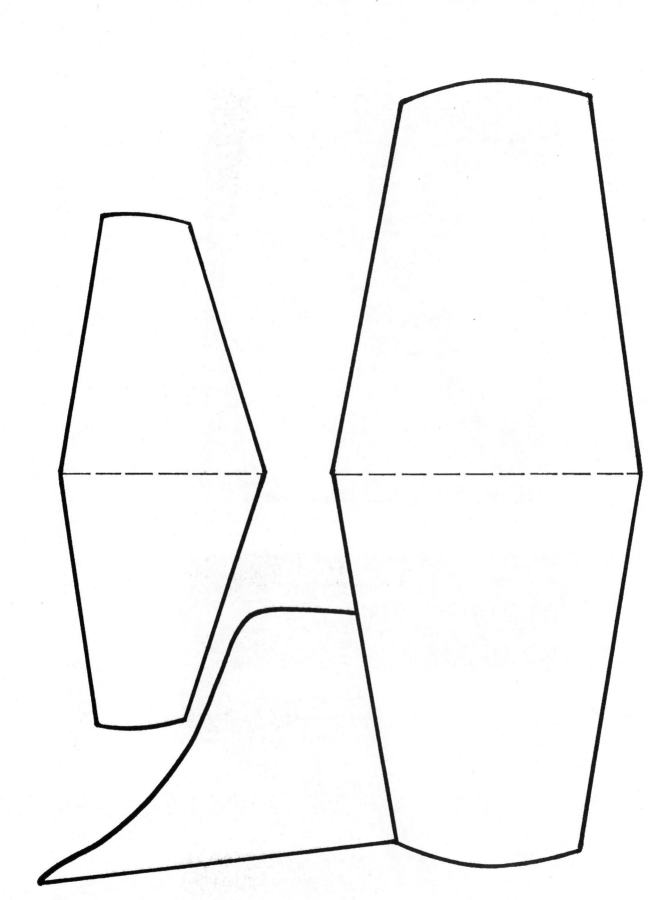

8-3 *Template for the X-1.*

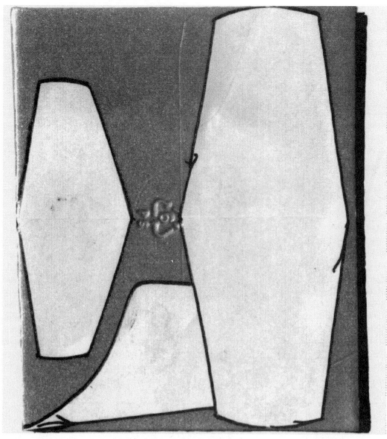

8-4 *The template is first outlined on the meat tray.*

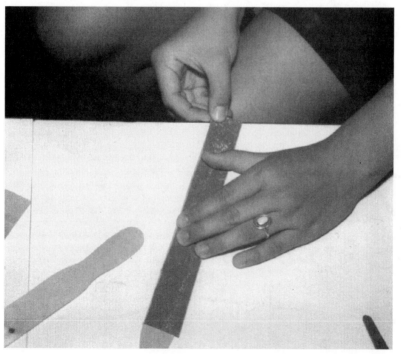

8-5 *The stick should look like this when completed.*

8-6 *The basic construction of Yeager's X-1. The wings*
are glued to the fuselage, the fin is glued to the
fuselage, the egg is shaped and glued to the nose, and
the stabilizers are glued to the fin.

8. Using the fin as your guide, hot-glue the left wing first. The wing should be perpendicular to the fin.

9. Hot-glue the left stabilizer to the fin. It should be aligned to the wing and the fin. It should be perpendicular to the fin and parallel to the wing. Again, use the blowup diagram as a guide.

10. Now glue the right wing and right stabilizer into their correct positions. Each should be aligned to the other and perpendicular to the fin.

11. Using your sanding stick, sand the lower part of the foam egg so that a portion of it fits into the pipe insulation (Figs. 8-7 and 8-8).

12. Once you have dry fitted the nose cone and it makes a nice, smooth front piece for the X-1's main body or fuselage, hot-glue it into place.

13. Hot-glue the soda straw into place on the top of the fuselage right beside the fin.

14. What a cool airplane! Ah, to make it more realistic, let's paint it bright orange. I used Testor's "Competition Orange" model paint (Fig. 8-9). Be careful. Some household paints will destroy the Styrofoam. Use only

First to exceed the speed of sound

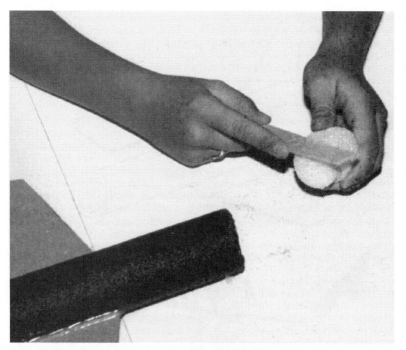

8-7 *The nose cone of the X-1 is shaped to fit into the foam fuselage tube. Once it fits snugly, use hot glue to make it stay in place.*

8-8 *After sanding, this is what the styrofoam "egg" should look like to make it a nose for the X-1 and the X-15.*

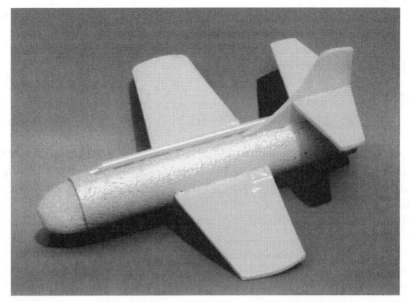

8-9 The X-1 finished, painted, and ready to fly.

hobby paints. Let the model dry thoroughly before trying to fly it. Hey! It'll look great!

E. Flying your plane

1. Your plane can be flown by hand as a glider.

2. It can also be powered as a rocket using a balloon.
   a. Run the string through the straw. Attach the string to something at each end so that it is stretched taut and more or less level.
   b. Inflate a balloon and hold it closed while attaching it to the bottom of the plane with masking tape. The opening of the balloon should point toward the rear of the plane.
   c. When you release the plane, it will zoom away.

F. Investigations

1. Using your plane as a glider, try holding it at different places when you launch. Where is the best location? What happens if you hold it back too far? What happens if you hold it too close to the nose?

2. Compare different angles of launch. Do you get a better flight if you hold the plane horizontal or if you point it somewhat upwards?

3. Try putting different amounts of air in the balloon. Does more air make it go further? Is there a minimum amount of air required to make it move at all?

4. Try tying the finish-line end of the string higher than the other end. Can your plane climb a hill? Is there a limit to how high the hill can be?

First to exceed the speed of sound

5. Try different kinds of string (or yarn or thread or fishing line). Does it change how far the plane is able to go?

Classroom connections

A. Science

1. Before flying the balloon-powered X-1s, you might want to experiment with just balloons on a string. You will need some additional straws and long balloons. Run a string or fishing line through the straw. Attach the line so that it is stretched taut between two points 15–20 feet apart. Inflate a long balloon and attach to the straw with tape. Release the balloon and see it fly. Repeat the procedure, measuring the length of the inflated balloon and timing how long it takes to get to the end. Try different amounts of air in the balloon. Does the time change? Does the distance traveled change? Discuss with the students what makes the balloon move. When the balloon is held closed, the air particles in the balloon are pushing evenly against the inside walls of the balloon. Everything is in equilibrium and the balloon does not move. When the balloon is released, the forces inside the balloon are no longer in equilibrium. There are still forces pushing on the front and sides of the balloon, but the backwards forces are eliminated. The air particles that would have pushed on the back of the balloon now escape instead. The result is that the car moves forward due to the unbalanced force in that direction.

2. Now repeat your experiments with the X-1. Being sure to compare flights with the balloon inflated to the same length. Which completes its flight in less time, the X-1 model or a single balloon? Can you think of an explanation for your results?

3. Encourage the students to try varying the type of string and track angle as described in the "Investigations" section.

B. Mathematics

1. I wish I had a nickel for every time I've heard a student moan, "I can do the calculations; I just can't do the word problems." Here are some word problems related to Yeager's flights for your students to practice on.
   a. The first flight in which Yeager broke the sound barrier traveled at a speed of 662 miles per hour. Six years later, he set a new record traveling at 1,650 miles per hour. Calculate the difference in speed for these two flights. How many times larger was the second speed than the first?
   b. The United States is approximately 2,807 miles from the East Coast to the West Coast. If you were traveling in the original X-1, how long would it take to fly from coast to coast?
   c. Imagine you are now traveling in the X-1A, the one Chuck Yeager flew to a speed of 1,650 miles per hour. How long would it take you to fly from coast to coast in this rocket plane?
   d. Which flight would take longer, the X-1 or the X-1A? How much longer?

e. Lindbergh's flight across the Atlantic was 3,614 miles and took 33.5 hours. How long would it have taken in the X-1?

C. Social studies

1. During World War II, the U.S. military was still segregated. However, for the first time black soldiers were allowed to train as fighter pilots. These airmen who trained at Tuskegee Army Airfield in Alabama essentially belonged to a separate black air force. They flew in the Allied campaigns in Europe and North Africa and developed a reputation for effectiveness. Their success helped ease hostilities between blacks and whites in the military. In 1948, President Harry Truman signed the order requiring desegregation of the U.S. military. Students can read more about these and other black pilots in *Black Eagles: African Americans in Aviation* by Jim Haskins.

2. Although not officially part of the military, women pilots also flew in World War II as part of the Women Airforce Service Pilots (WASPs). They ferried planes, tested new aircraft, flew at night so radar operators could practice tracking them, and towed targets behind their planes for student antiaircraft gunners to shoot at (not a particularly safe job). The director of the WASPs was Jackie Cochran. Her life story is full of determination to succeed. She never knew her parents and lived with a foster family in Florida and Georgia. The family was extremely poor, and Jackie started working in a cotton mill at age eight to help feed the family. Through her early life she worked up through a series of better-paying jobs. In her early 20s, she took a job as a sales representative and took up flying to save driving time between customers. She fell in love with flying. Over the next 40 years, she would set many speed records. In 1953, she was the first woman to break the sound barrier, and in the process broke the previous speed record for men or women. Chuck Yeager, whom you met in this chapter, was her coach in flying jet aircraft as she prepared for this feat. Interested students can read more about her life in *At the Controls: Women in Aviation* by Carole Briggs. Also in this book are the stories of Jerrie Cobb, the first of 12 women to pass the astronaut test for the Mercury program (unfortunately, NASA decided not to accept women into the program); Sheila Scott, the first person to fly a light aircraft over the North Pole; and Bonnie Tiburzi, who in 1973 became the first woman pilot hired by a major airline.

D. Language arts

1. When Yeager broke the sound barrier, it did not become public knowledge until eight months later. Can you imagine keeping a secret for eight months? Write about a secret or surprise you were asked to keep for a long time and how you were able to accomplish it. Describe how you felt and if you really wanted to share your excitement with friends and family. Read your paper to a friend or a partner.

2. With a partner, brainstorm words associated with flight. Then write a list of rhyming words related to your brainstormed list. Use these words to construct an original poem about the accomplishment of Chuck Yeager.

First to exceed the speed of sound

3. It can be very frightening to be the first to try something. Have you ever been the first to try a new game, sport, or other activity? Were you afraid of failing or being made fun of? In a small group, discuss ways group members have found the courage to try new things.

4. If you were the first to accomplish something, would you like everyone to make a big deal about it, or would you prefer to enjoy the satisfaction in a private way with just friends and family recognizing your accomplishment? Why do you feel this way? Describe your feelings to another person.

5. Students can learn more about Yeager in *Chuck Yeager, The Man Who Broke the Sound Barrier*, by Nancy Levinson, or *Chuck Yeager, The First Man to Fly Faster Than Sound*, by Timothy Gaffney.

First to fly into space

9

Scott Crossfield's X-15, 1960

Albert Scott Crossfield was born in Berkeley, California, on October 2, 1921. He was bedridden as a child with bouts of rheumatic fever and pneumonia. During this time he became interested in reading about pilots and airplanes. He was able to begin flying lessons when he was 13 years old. He delivered papers to the pilot in exchange for the lessons. He was a Naval aviator in World War II and flew the famous Corsair fighter.

He went back to college after the war and attained a Master of Science degree in aeronautical engineering. Scott continued flying and became a civilian test pilot. In 1953, he was the first human to exceed twice the speed of sound in an airplane called the Douglas Skyrocket.

Even before the beginning of the National Aeronautics and Space Administration (NASA), there was a great deal of interest in space flight.

9-1 *First to fly into space: Scott Crossfield's X-15.*

The U.S. government wanted to test a variety of theories about flying in space. Scott worked for a company then known as North American and was eventually selected to test fly their X-15 (Fig. 9-1). This aircraft was designed to fly up into space and return to land at an airfield back on Earth. The X-15 could fly in the atmosphere or in space. This was the beginning of true aerospace flight. During his test missions in the X-15, Scott routinely flew into the edge of space and back. He is considered by many aviation historians to be the world's first true astronaut. The knowledge gained in testing the X-15 led to the success of the current Space Shuttle.

Fast facts

❑ There is a road at Edwards Air Force Base in California named "Crossfield Pike." It is named after Scott Crossfield. He once ran out of space when he landed on the dry lake bed and ended up on a county road.

❑ The X-15 set a speed record of 4,534 miles per hour that stood until it was broken by the Space Shuttle in 1981.

❑ NACA was the forerunner of NASA. The Skyrocket and the X-15 were developed under the administration of NACA, or the National Advisory Commission on Aeronautics.

❑ All NACA pilots were engineers, some with several degrees. These pilots shared in the design and engineering of the aircraft they eventually flew.

❑ Mr. and Mrs. Crossfield had six children, and they retired to live in Herndon, Virginia.

❑ Crossfield is still an active pilot and owns a Cessna 210 (Fig. 9-2).

9-2
A. Scott Crossfield, 1995.

Project 9

You build it—
Scott Crossfield's X-15

A. The basic materials

1. Foam pipe insulation 14 inches long and 2 inches in diameter will be needed for the fuselage.

2. The nose cone will be made from a Styrofoam "egg." This foam egg can be found at craft stores nationwide. The egg should be about 2 inches in diameter and 2 inches long.

3. Meat trays from supermarkets make perfect "wings" and tail surfaces. You need one that gives you about 9¼ inches × 7½ inches of working area. This is the "working bottom" of the tray. Or you could use several smaller ones.

4. A flat stick, like a stirring stick from a paint store.

5. A piece of medium to fine sandpaper.

6. (Optional) a pencil and a good-size (#64) rubber band.

B. Tools

1. Large scissors will be needed to cut the foam trays.

2. A hot glue gun is a must to make the foam tray material stick to the foam pipe insulation.

C. Safety precautions

1. Always be careful when cutting with scissors.

2. Hot glue guns can burn you if you get careless, so don't get in a hurry. Be sure to unplug it when you're through.

3. Even though the X-15 has a soft foam nose, it can still hurt someone if thrown or projected. Fly it in open areas away from small children and pets.

D. Steps of construction

1. Make a copy of the template page on a copy machine. This will save the book from damage. Using the template provided, cut out the wings, fin, and stabilizers as described in the following (Fig. 9-3).

First to fly into space

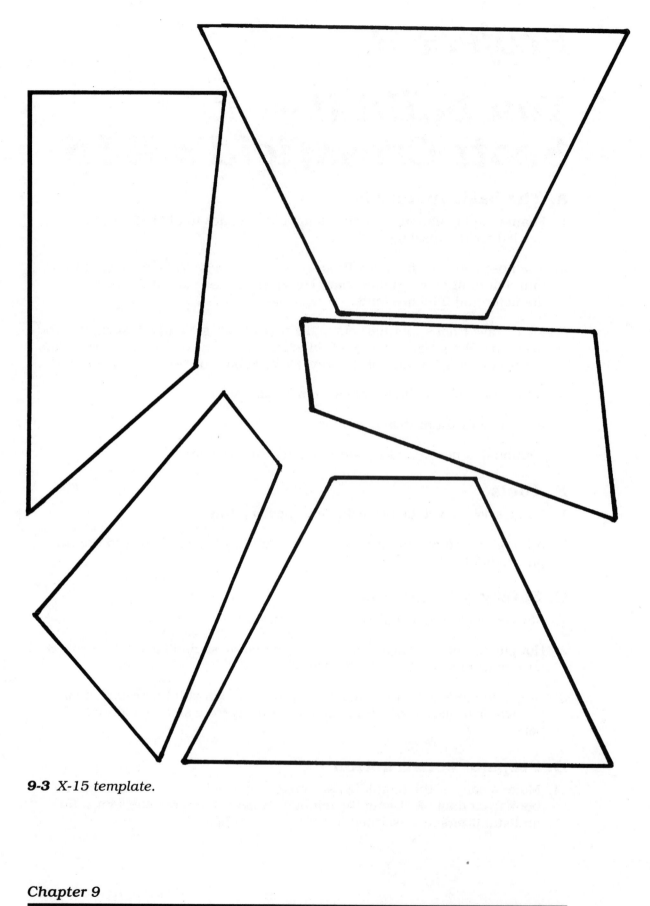

9-3 X-15 template.

9-4
After the template is transferred to the meat tray, carefully cut out the parts to the X-15.

2. Put the templates down on the "working bottom" of the foam meat tray and either trace the wings, fin, and stabilizer outlines or rubber cement them to the tray (Fig. 9-4).

3. Using large scissors, cut out the wings, fin, and stabilizers.

4. Glue a piece of sandpaper approximately 4 inches long to a flat stick, like a stirring stick from a paint store. Using this sanding stick, sand the edges of the wings, stabilizers, and fin where they will bond to the fuselage. You need to create a nice flat edge (Figs. 9-5, 9-6, 9-7).

5. Using the blowup diagram (Fig. 9-8) or the photograph (Fig. 9-9) as a guide, hot-glue the fin first to the fuselage.

6. Using the fin as your guide, hot-glue the left wing first (Fig. 9-10). The wing should be perpendicular to the fin (Fig. 9-11).

7. Hot-glue the left stabilizer to the fuselage. It should be directly behind the wing and tilted slightly below the wing again, use the blowup diagram as a guide. Now glue the right wing and right stabilizer into their correct positions.

8. Using your sanding stick, sand the foam nose cone so that the center portion of it fits snugly into the nose cone (Fig. 9-12). Skip down and read steps 11–14 before continuing. If you decide to add the rubber band, leave out steps 9 and 10.

First to fly into space

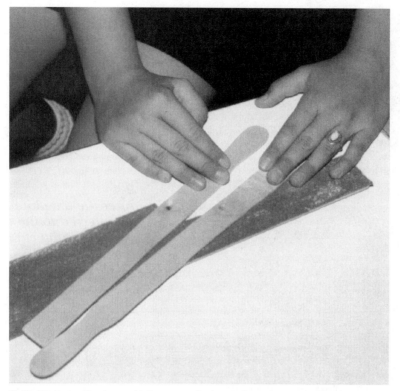

9-5 *Paint stirring sticks can be made into sanding sticks.*

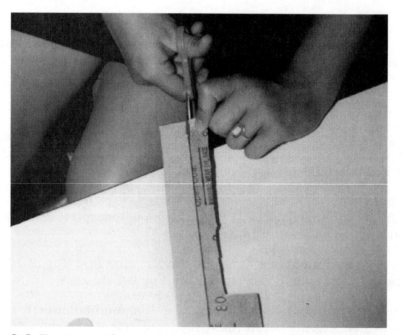

9-6 *First coat the stirring stick with glue. Then place the back side of a piece of medium sandpaper on the stirring stick. Cut the sandpaper to the edge of the stick.*

9-7
Using the stirring stick with sandpaper glued to it, sand the edges to make a uniform surface for attachment.

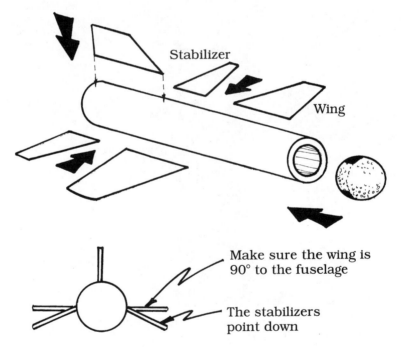

Stabilizer

Wing

Make sure the wing is 90° to the fuselage

The stabilizers point down

9-8 *The wings are glued to the fuselage. The fin glued to the fuselage, and the egg is shaped and glued to the nose. The stabilizers are then glued at angles to the fuselage.*

First to fly into space

9-9 *The X-15 with a tapered "cone" nose.*

9-10 *Apply hot glue to the foam fuselage where the wings will be attached.*

9. Once you have fitted the nose cone and it makes a nice smooth front piece for the X-15's main body, or fuselage, hot-glue it into place. Once the glue dries, you are ready to fly (Fig. 9-13).

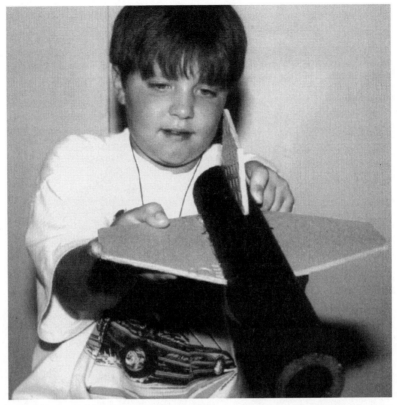

9-11 *Make sure that the wings are properly aligned.*

9-12 *Remove enough styrofoam from the egg to make it fit.*

9-13 *Once the nose cone fits the foam tube, you can glue it and make your X-15 hand launched or you can punch a hole through the egg and push a rubber band through it to make the X-15 power launched.*

10. You might find that the glider needs nose weight. Here's a way to add it: Stand your X-15 on its nose. Dribble several drops of white glue (like Elmer's) down the inside of the fuselage so that it collects on the Styrofoam of the nose cone. Then drop in a couple of pennies so they rest in the puddle of glue. Let this dry for an hour or two. The pennies will become embedded in the glue and stay there during flight tests. That should make the X-15 fly better.

11. Here is an optional method for launching your X-15. Before inserting the nose cone, poke a pencil through it (parallel to the fuselage, not across it). Using the eraser end, carefully stuff your rubber band through the nose cone so that it sticks out on both sides. Using a piece of wood, plastic, or a paper clip, secure the rubber band on the end that goes into the fuselage.

12. Hot-glue your securing stick along with the rubber band to the Styrofoam. Let this dry and cool thoroughly.

13. Hot-glue the nose cone into the foam fuselage.

14. You now have a means of launching your X-15 other than by hand. The only problem with this is eventually it will wear away at the Styrofoam nose cone. If this happens, make another one and reglue it to the X-15.

Here's a top-secret tip: A 35-mm plastic film can, with its cover on, will slip neatly into the tail of the X-15. This makes a secret hiding place for valuables. Or you can put more goodies into the fuselage of the X-15 and plug the tail end with your film can. Cool, huh? But remember to remove your treasures before flying!

E. Flying your plane

1. Your plane can be flown by hand as a glider.

2. If you attached the rubber band, you can also use it to launch the plane. Launch the X-15 by catching the rubber band on the index finger of your left hand and pulling the plane back with your right hand. Release the plane. You should vary the amount you stretch the rubber band and the angle at which you hold the plane until you achieve a smooth launch.

3. Imagine flying your plane up into space and back as Scott Crossfield did!

F. Investigations

1. Practice launching your X-15 with the rubber band until you can get a smooth launch almost every time. Now start trying to find what variables affect the flight of the plane. First, try changing the amount you stretch the rubber band without changing the way you hold the plane. Does stretching the rubber band more always make the plane go farther?

2. Now try to change the angle at which you hold the plane while using the same amount of stretch each time. Does this change the flight? What about where you hold the plane?

3. When scientists do an experiment like this investigating one thing at a time while trying to keep everything else the same, they say they are "controlling variables." This is always good scientific procedure. If you change several things at once, you won't know what caused the effect you observe.

Classroom connections

A. Science

1. Divide the class into small groups and have each group build an X-15 model including the optional rubber band launcher. You might want to have them make extra nose cones in case of disaster during the experiment. Allow time for everyone in the group to try launching the rocket a few times, then ask each group to select its best "launcher." These "launchers" should practice until they can achieve a consistent launch. You might allow them to practice during recess the day before you plan to do the experiment. The goal of the experiment is to determine how the amount the rubber band is stretched affects the flight of the rocket. Have the students measure the distance from launch point to landing point for several different lengths of the stretched rubber band. Each case should be repeated several times, and the rest of the group should watch the launcher to make sure that other things like launch angle and the position in which the rocket is held are as consistent as possible. Lots of things can

affect the flight so repeated trials will probably not give exactly the same distance. Nevertheless, students should be able to tell that more stretch means greater distance. Discuss the reason for this with the students. If they have previously studied energy, give them a chance to develop an explanation in their small groups before having the class discussion. When you stretch the rubber band, you are doing work that transfers energy to the rubber band. The more it is stretched, the more energy is stored. This stored energy is called *elastic potential energy*. It is "potential" energy because the rubber band now has the potential to make the rocket move. When you release the rocket, the rubber band contracts, converting its stored energy into motion, or "kinetic," energy of the rocket. The more energy the rocket has, the faster it travels, and thus the farther it goes before it hits the ground.

2. This is a great place to discuss experiment design and control of variables with your students. *How to Think Like a Scientist* by Stephen Kramer discusses these topics by telling stories requiring solutions to questions. The questions are answered through the process of formulating a hypothesis and testing it using experiments involving control of variables. You might want to read the book to the class and involve them in the story by discussing what should be done before the characters decide how to approach the problem.

B. Mathematics

1. When carrying out the experiment described previously, encourage your students to use metric units of measurement: centimeters for the rubber band stretch and meters for the flight. You might want to do a general review of metric units at this point. Scientists all over the world use the metric system. The United States is the only major country still using the English system of units. We have used it with some reluctance in this book because when you go to the hardware store to buy pipe insulation, it is labeled as 1-inch diameter, not 2.5-centimeter diameter.

2. Converting units is good practice for developing understanding of the fundamental meaning of multiplication and division. Here are some more word problems for your students to practice on.

   a. One mile equals 5,280 feet and 1,610 meters. The X-15 eventually flew 354,000 feet above the Earth. How high is this in miles? How high is it in meters? How many kilometers is this? (Remember, 1 kilometer is 1,000 meters.)

   b. The speed of sound in air is 760 miles per hour. How many meters per hour is this?

   c. The X-15 set a speed record of 4,534 miles per hour. How far could it travel in one minute? How far could it travel in one second?

   d. According to the *Guinness Book of World Records*, the fastest that humans have ever traveled is 24,791 miles per hour, which was reached during Apollo X's flight back to the Earth from the Moon. If they had continued at this speed, how far would they have traveled in a day? (Another way of asking the same question is, "What was their speed in miles per day?")

C. Social studies

1. Scott Crossfield first flew into space in 1960. The late 1950s and early 1960s were a very interesting time in America. In 1957, the USSR launched the Sputnik satellite, and the space race began. The civil rights movement was just getting started. The "cold" war threatened to become a "hot" one as tensions between the U.S. and USSR increased over the placement of missiles in Cuba. Talk to your parents or grandparents about what events of this era stand out in their memories.

2. Read about other speed records in the *Guinness Book of World Records*. The topics covered in this book vary from year to year. The 1990 edition has a variety of material related to speed records, from fastest airliners to fastest insects to fastest glaciers.

3. We have talked mostly about pilots, but there are many careers in aviation that don't involve flying an airplane. Brainstorm some of these occupations, such as air traffic controller, baggage handler, aeronautical engineer, and mechanic. Divide the class into groups to investigate what some of these people do and the training required for their jobs. Older students might enjoy reading *Breakthrough: Women in Aviation*, which profiles nine contemporary women in aviation careers, ranging from air traffic controller to aviation inspector to astronaut.

D. Language arts

1. A roller-coaster ride can offer you the thrill of riding at high speeds. What sensations do you experience as you travel up and down at a high speed? How does your body react? What emotions do you experience? Would you repeat the ride? Why or why not? Write an essay describing your experiences.

2. Write a paragraph describing what you think it would be like to be a test pilot.

3. Have you ever gone to an arcade and played a game where you were the pilot flying a very fast airplane? Write a persuasive paragraph telling someone else why he or she should also have this experience.

4. Scott Crossfield once said, "There is no divine assignment to those who do things. The opportunity is for all and probably within the grasp of most." Choose one of the following related themes for a class discussion or writing assignment:
    a. Crossfield believes that most people can do whatever they set their minds to. Have you ever had an idea that you continued working on until you achieved the results that you were looking for?
    b. It is important to not be discouraged with your ideas. Some people might tell you that your idea is not worthwhile and you should just give up. What would you say to these people? How do you feel when you are able to accomplish something that someone told you was impossible?

The father of space flight

10

Robert H. Goddard, 1929

Robert Goddard was born in Worcester, Massachusetts. He was always interested in rocket science, and as he grew up, he kept thinking about rockets and their fuel. The experiments he did between 1901 and 1945 were invaluable to the development of space science. Eventually this led to the missiles and rockets used in our defense and for space exploration (Fig. 10-1).

Dr. Goddard published a report in 1919 called "A Method of Reaching Extreme Altitudes." He used this report to describe the kind of rocket flight he thought could be used to reach the moon. Most scientists at that time didn't take him seriously. He quietly continued to work, and most of his work didn't become recognized until after his death.

10-1 *Robert H. Goddard: The father of space flight.*

In 1926, near Auburn, Massachusetts, Dr. Goddard successfully launched the world's first liquid-propelled rocket. This is the kind of fuel that was used in the Saturn Moon rocket that put man on the moon in 1969, and it's the kind of fuel system that powers the Space Shuttle.

Goddard's 1929 liquid-propelled rocket carried instruments, including a barometer, a thermometer, and a small camera. Because he needed a large, open area to work on his rockets, Dr. Goddard moved his family to New Mexico. His wife, Ester, made home movies of his experiments, and these give scientific proof of his successes and failures.

Some of his experiments included a rocket that reached a speed of 550 miles per hour and went as high as 1½ miles. The Germans used much of his work as the basis for the development of their war missiles. During World War II, Goddard helped the U.S. Navy develop jet and rocket-assisted takeoff motors for seaplanes.

Robert Goddard's work was the beginning of human space exploration. During his life, he received little attention from his country and his fellow scientists; however, after his death, the government recognized his contribution, and his family was awarded a Congressional Gold Medal.

Fast facts

❏ A rocket engine that is the same size as an automobile engine produces approximately 3,000 times more power.

❏ The first solid-fueled rockets were developed by the Chinese, but it was not until Goddard developed the liquid-fueled rocket that humans were able to leave the Earth.

❏ The British army used solid-fueled rockets in the battle against Fort McHenry during the War of 1812. Francis Scott Key described the "rocket's red glare" in a poem he wrote about the battle, which later became the Star Spangled Banner, our national anthem.

❏ Goddard holds 214 patents for his work in rocketry.

❏ Charles Lindbergh assisted Goddard with his first grant from the Guggenheim Foundation.

❏ The mixture of gasoline and liquid oxygen developed by Goddard for his liquid-fueled rocket was the same as that used by NASA 35 years later to put men into space.

Project 10a

You build it—The indoor rocket launch

A "RamRocket" launcher (Fig. 10-2) will be used to launch your model rockets. This is a wonderful method of launching foam models indoors. The RamRocket costs $11.95 and can be purchased from Chasco Toys, P.O. Box 128, Duncan, Oklahoma 73534-0128. A foam rocket that is part of the RamRocket package is already assembled and ready to fly. Use this first to become familiar with the operation of the launcher, then you'll be ready to fly your own rockets.

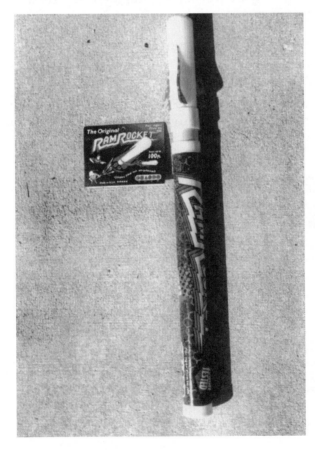

10-2
The RamRocket launcher. This works great for indoor rocket launching. The Chasco Company makes soft foam rockets that fly a long distance by compressed-air launching. To inquire, write Chasco Toys, P.O. Box 128, Duncan, Oklahoma 73534-0128.

A. The basic materials

1. A tube of 1-inch (inside diameter) foam tubing that is used for insulating pipes. This can be found at hardware and building-supply centers.

2. Meat trays made of Styrofoam.

The father of space flight

3. Styrofoam eggs slightly larger than the foam tubing. (Found in craft stores.)

4. A stirring stick like those used in paint stores.

5. A piece of medium to fine sandpaper.

6. White glue (used for sanding stick only).

B. Tools

1. Scissors.

2. A hot glue gun.

C. Safety precautions

1. Always be careful when cutting with scissors.

2. Hot glue guns can burn you if you get careless, so don't get in a hurry. Be sure to unplug it when you're through.

3. Never launch your rocket directly towards anyone.

D. Steps of construction

1. Using the rocket that came with the launcher (Fig. 10-3) as a guide, cut rocket fins out of the meat tray. You have enough experience with this now that you can be creative.

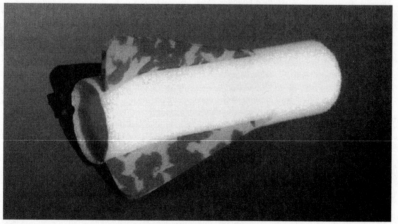

10-3 *The RamRocket indoor rocket. You can fly this one or, using the same plan as the X-1 or X-15, you can make your own.*

2. Cut the foam tubing to a length of about 8 inches.

3. Plug in the hot glue gun and let it warm up.

4. Using the original rocket as a guide for placement, glue the fins to the body of the rocket.

5. Make a sanding stick like the one used in chapter 8 to build Yeager's X-1. The sandpaper can be glued to the stick with white glue like Elmer's.

6. Using the sanding stick, round off the back of a Styrofoam egg so that it fits into the foam tubing.

7. Hot glue the Styrofoam egg into the rocket's body. It is important to get a tight seal all the way around.

E. Flying your rocket

1. Mount your rocket onto the RamRocket launcher (Fig. 10-4) and let it fly. Remember, don't point it at anyone, and always launch in an open area. If you are launching indoors, don't hold on to the rocket, and only pull the launcher out about halfway. Try not to hit lamps, vases, and pictures hanging on walls. The impact of the rocket can knock things down.

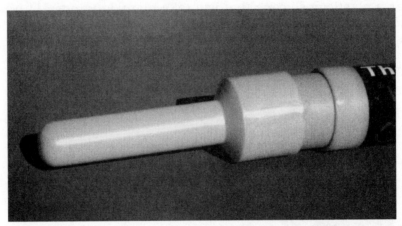

10-4 *This is the launching end of the RamRocket.*

2. If you are launching outdoors, the rocket can be made to soar as high as 100 feet. Follow the directions on the launcher. It might take a few tries to learn just the right time to release the rocket, but once you have mastered the technique, the result is awesome.

F. Investigations

1. Does the speed with which you close the launcher make a difference in how high the rocket goes? Can you explain this? (Hint: Listen carefully.)

2. In a large, open area like a playground, try launching the rocket horizontally. Use something to mark where you stood for the launch and where the rocket landed. Now try launching it at an angle. Did it go farther this time? Can you find an angle that gives the maximum range?

3. Skip over to the "Science" part of "Classroom connections" and read about how your RamRocket works.

Project 10b

You build it—The outdoor rocket launch

Model rocketry has become a fascinating hobby for young and old. The models that you can buy are easy to build, safe to fly, and relatively inexpensive. For a first project and flight, it is recommended that young people, and adults for that matter, start with an easy model that will give great success. The Estes model, known as the Gnome (Fig. 10-5), is a perfect beginner's rocket. It has fins that are made of plastic and ready to mount on a simple body tube (Fig. 10-6). It has a plastic nose cone that will take many landings. With permission of Estes Industries, the instruction sheet (Fig. 10-7) has been reprinted here so you can study it before buying, building, and flying the model.

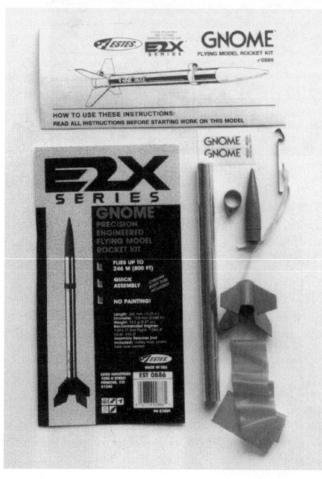

10-5
The Gnome Rocket by Estes Industries.

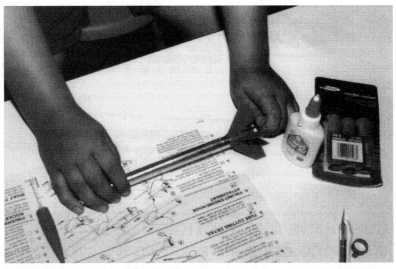

10-6 *The Gnome is easy to build and fun to fly, again and again.*

Once you've studied the instruction sheet, you will have an idea of what's involved in building the Gnome. There are hundreds of teachers throughout the United States who have built and flown model rockets in elementary classes.

The Gnome should only be launched outdoors, since it will go up several hundred feet. To launch the rocket, you can buy an Estes launcher or build a launcher with materials you can obtain at building-supply and hardware stores. Use the instructions that follow. It's simple, inexpensive, and easy to use for one launch or hundreds.

A. The basic materials

1. A piece of plywood or other board that is approximately 12 inches × 12 inches. This doesn't have to be exact, but it should not be significantly smaller (Fig. 10-8).

2. A piano wire or welding rod that is 36 inches long × ⅛ inch.

3. Standard electrical two-strand cord. This is like the cord that lamps and other electrical appliances have. A length of 15 feet should work well.

4. Two screw-type "alligator clips" (Fig. 10-9). These can be purchased at hardware stores and specialty shops like Radio Shack (so can the electrical cord).

5. A 6-volt lantern battery.

The plywood, welding rod, electrical wire, and 6-volt lantern battery were purchased at a local building supply center for about $9.00.

ESTES INDUSTRIES
1295 H STREET
PENROSE, CO 81240 USA

GNOME™

FLYING MODEL ROCKET KIT
#0886

HOW TO USE THESE INSTRUCTIONS:

READ ALL INSTRUCTIONS BEFORE STARTING WORK ON THIS MODEL

A. This rocket, incorporating basic model rocketry construction techniques, will help you in the development of your rocketry modeling skills.

B. **Read each step first** and visualize the procedure thoroughly in your mind before starting construction.

C. Lay parts out on the table in front of you. (Check inside tubes for any small parts.)

D. Use exploded view to match all parts contained in kit.

E. Collect all construction supplies that are not included in the kit.

F. Test fit parts before applying any glue.

G. The construction supplies required for each step are listed at the beginning of each step.

H. Check off each step as you complete it.

EXPLODED VIEW

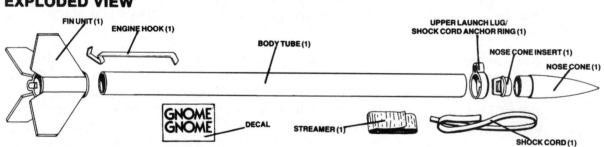

FIN UNIT (1) ENGINE HOOK (1) BODY TUBE (1) UPPER LAUNCH LUG/ SHOCK CORD ANCHOR RING (1) NOSE CONE INSERT (1) NOSE CONE (1) DECAL STREAMER (1) SHOCK CORD (1)

EXTREMELY IMPORTANT: THE EXPLODED VIEW IS FOR REFERENCE ONLY! DO NOT USE THIS DRAWING ALONE TO ASSEMBLE THIS MODEL.

The exploded view is only intended to assist you in locating the parts included in this kit. Refer back to this exploded view as you build your model step by step. This method will help you to put the parts into perspective as you progress through the construction.

CONSTRUCTION SUPPLIES

In addition to the parts included in your kit, you will need these construction supplies. Each step shows which supplies will be required.

 SCISSORS   HOBBY KNIFE   PENCIL   PLASTIC CEMENT   MASKING TAPE

GLUE IS APPLIED TO SURFACES SHOWN IN RED.

10-7 *Instructions for building the Gnome.*

1. NOSE CONE ASSEMBLY

A. ☐ **Test fit** the nose cone insert into the nose cone. **Do not glue at this time.** Remove the insert.

B. ☐ Apply plastic cement as shown in the illustration and assemble the nose cone and insert pieces. Allow assembly to dry.

2. TUBE MARKING DETAIL

A. ☐ Using a door frame as a guide, draw a straight line along the entire length of the tube.

B. ☐ Locate the ruler printed in the center crease of this instruction sheet.

C. ☐ Lay one end of the body tube on the zero mark of the ruler.

D. ☐ Place three marks on the line you drew in step 2A. Make two marks 38 mm (1 ½") from each end of the tube. Make a third mark at 10 mm (3/8") from zero. Make this mark 13 mm (1/2") long.

3. TUBE CUTTING DETAIL

A. ☐ Cut a 3 mm (1/8") wide slit at the two 38 mm (1½) marks as shown. **Do not cut a slot at the 10 mm (3/8") mark.**

4. FIN UNIT/ENGINE HOOK ATTACHMENT

NOTE: Inspect the fin unit for the launch lug and engine hook slot.

A. ☐ Slide the fin unit onto the body tube and position it about halfway along the tube. Orient the engine hook slot over the line you drew in step 2A.

B. ☐ Insert one end of the engine hook into the slit on the end of the tube with the 10 mm (3/8") mark as shown.

C. ☐ Test fit by sliding fin unit over the engine hook.

D. ☐ Make sure hook fits into slot on fin unit.

E. ☐ Slide fin unit halfway up tube.

F. ☐ Apply tube-type plastic cement around the body tube in a "zigzag" fashion as shown in the illustration.

G. ☐ Push the fin unit down the tube and over the engine hook. Continue pushing until the rear of the fin unit touches the 10 mm (3/8") mark. Carefully wipe away any excess plastic cement.

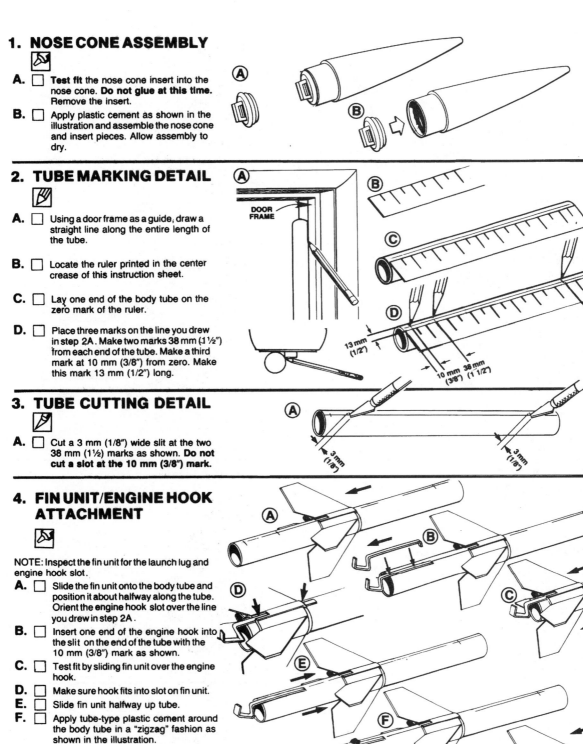

Page 2

10-7 Continued.

5. SHOCK CORD MOUNT ATTACHMENT

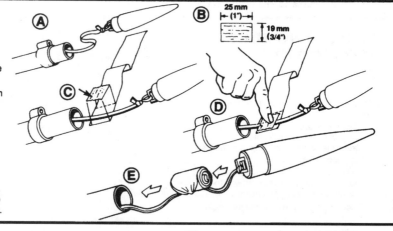

NOTE: The shock cord mount ring performs two functions.
1. It holds the shock cord in place.
2. Acts as the forward launch lug.
The forward launch lug must be in line with the fin unit launch lug for proper fit on the launch rod.

A. ☐ Inspect the launch lug ring for the shock cord slot and launch lug using the illustration to the right.

B. ☐ Use a modeling knife or pencil to push one end of the shock cord into the forward slot.

C. ☐ Pull the shock cord through the slot and out the forward end of the body tube leaving 6 mm (1/4") exposed as shown.

D. ☐ Test fit the launch lug ring by sliding it over the front of the tube. Orient the slot over the line as you did with fin unit and push over the shock cord.

E. ☐ Make sure the cord fits into the slot on the inside of the ring. Now remove ring.

F. ☐ Spread a band of plastic cement around the body tube just behind the protruding shock cord.

G. ☐ Position the launch lug ring on the body tube noting the shock cord slot. Push the ring over the shock cord until the **forward edge** of the ring is even with the shock cord slot.

H. ☐ Erase pencil line on body tube with pencil eraser.

6. RECOVERY DEVICE ATTACHMENT

A. ☐ Tie free end of the shock cord to nose cone. Use a double knot.

B. ☐ Cut a 25 mm (1") long piece of 19 mm (3/4") wide masking tape.

C. ☐ Lay end of shock cord over end of streamer material as shown and tape shock and streamer together.

D. ☐ Press tape down firmly to assure a strong bond.

E. ☐ Roll streamer, insert streamer, shock cord and nose cone into Gnome™ body. Recovery device should slide easily into body tube. If too tight, unfold and repack.

7. FINISHING YOUR ROCKET

When all glue is completely dry, apply self-adhesive decals. Cut out each decal inside dashed line, apply on model and press down.

WHAT TO EXPECT WHEN FLYING YOUR GNOME™ ROCKET

The Gnome™ is easy to build and fly. The streamer recovery allows for safe recovery on small fields. With the largest engine you can use with the Gnome, the A3-4T, you can expect about 244 meters (800 feet) in altitude. The 1/2A3-2T should deliver about 122 meters (400 feet). The A3-4T will work fine on football fields while the 1/2A3-4T would be perfect for baseball fields.

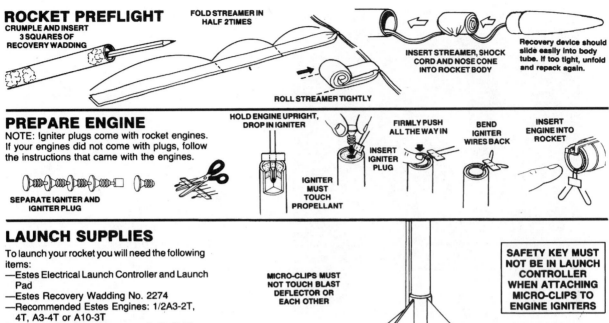

ROCKET PREFLIGHT
CRUMPLE AND INSERT
3 SQUARES OF
RECOVERY WADDING

FOLD STREAMER IN
HALF 2 TIMES

ROLL STREAMER TIGHTLY

INSERT STREAMER, SHOCK
CORD AND NOSE CONE
INTO ROCKET BODY

Recovery device should
slide easily into body
tube. If too tight, unfold
and repack again.

PREPARE ENGINE
NOTE: Igniter plugs come with rocket engines.
If your engines did not come with plugs, follow
the instructions that came with the engines.

SEPARATE IGNITER AND
IGNITER PLUG

HOLD ENGINE UPRIGHT,
DROP IN IGNITER

IGNITER
MUST
TOUCH
PROPELLANT

INSERT
IGNITER
PLUG

FIRMLY PUSH
ALL THE WAY IN

BEND
IGNITER
WIRES BACK

INSERT
ENGINE INTO
ROCKET

LAUNCH SUPPLIES
To launch your rocket you will need the following
items:
—Estes Electrical Launch Controller and Launch
  Pad
—Estes Recovery Wadding No. 2274
—Recommended Estes Engines: 1/2A3-2T,
  4T, A3-4T or A10-3T
To become familiar with your rocket's flight
pattern, use a 1/2A3-2T engine for your first flight.
Use only Estes products to launch this rocket.

MICRO-CLIPS MUST
NOT TOUCH BLAST
DEFLECTOR OR
EACH OTHER

**SAFETY KEY MUST
NOT BE IN LAUNCH
CONTROLLER
WHEN ATTACHING
MICRO-CLIPS TO
ENGINE IGNITERS**

FLYING YOUR ROCKET
Choose a large field away from power lines, tall
trees, and low flying aircraft. Try to find a field at
least 76 meters (250 feet) square. The larger the
launch area, the better your chance of recovering
your rocket. Football fields and playgrounds are
great.

Launch area must be free of dry weeds and
brown grass.

Launch only during calm weather with little or no
wind and good visibility.

COUNTDOWN AND LAUNCH

(10) BE CERTAIN SAFETY KEY IS NOT IN LAUNCH CONTROLLER.

(9) Remove safety cap and slide launch lug over launch rod to place rocket on
launch pad. Make sure the rocket slides freely on the launch rod.

(8) Attach micro-clips to the igniter wires. Arrange the clips so they do not touch
each other or the metal blast deflector. Attach clips as close to protective
tape on igniter as possible.

(7) Move back from your rocket as far as launch wire will permit (at least 5
meters - 15 feet).

(6) INSERT SAFETY KEY to arm the launch controller.

Give audible countdown 5...4...3...2...1

LAUNCH!!
PUSH AND HOLD LAUNCH BUTTON UNTIL ENGINE IGNITES

REMOVE SAFETY KEY FROM LAUNCH CONTROLLER. REPLACE SAFETY
KEY AND SAFETY CAP ON LAUNCH ROD.

MISFIRES
If the igniter functions properly but the propellant
does not ignite, keep in mind the following: An
Estes igniter will function properly even if the
coated tip is chipped. However, if the coated tip
is not in direct contact with the engine propellant,
it will only heat and not ignite the engine.

When an ignition failure occurs, remove the
safety key from the launch control system and
wait one minute before approaching the rocket.
Remove the expended igniter from the engine
and install a new one. Be certain the coated tip
is in direct contact with the engine propellant,
then reinstall the igniter plug as illustrated above.
Repeat the countdown and launch procedure.

**If you use the ultrasafe E2™ or Command™ Launch Controllers to fly your models,
use the following launch steps.**
A. After attaching micro-clips, etc., insert the safety key into the controller receptacle. If the
igniter clips have been attached properly to the igniter, the red L.E.D. will now begin to
flash on and off and the audio continuity indicator will beep on and off.
B. Hold the yellow (left) arm button down. The L.E.D. will stop flashing and the audio indicator
will produce a steady tone.
C. Verbally count down from five to zero loud enough for the bystanders to hear. Still holding
the yellow arm button down, push and hold the orange (right) button down until the rocket
ignites and lifts off.

FOR YOUR SAFETY AND ENJOYMENT
Always follow the NAR* MODEL ROCKETRY SAFETY CODE while participating in any model rocketry activities.

*National Association of Rocketry
Page 4

083888-2

10-7 Continued.

10-8
The piano wire, or welding rod, is what holds the rocket in place. The launch lugs slip over the rod.

10-9
Once in position, the alligator clips attach to the igniter wires.

B. Tools

1. An electric drill will be needed to drill a ⅛-inch hole in the center of the 12-inch × 12-inch square board.

2. A knife or a pair of side-cut pliers can be used to strip insulation from the electrical wire.

3. Small screwdriver.

C. Safety precautions

1. If using a knife to strip the wire, be very careful so you do not cut yourself. Never push the knife toward your hand.

2. Wear eye protection while using the electric drill and stripping the insulation.

3. Follow all safety instructions that came with your electric drill.

4. Launch your rocket only in a large area away from power lines.

5. The launch area should be free of dry weeds and brown grass.

6. Launch only on days with very little wind.

7. If the engine does not ignite, disconnect the wires from the battery and wait at least one minute before approaching the rocket. Reinstall the igniter and repeat the launch procedure.

D. Steps of construction

1. After the ⅛-inch hole is drilled into the center of the square board, the rod is inserted into the hole. The launch lug shown in the rocket instruction sheet slides down this rod, and the rocket will rest on the square board.

2. Separate the wire cord for about a foot back from each end.

3. Strip about ½ inch of the wire insulation on one end of the cord to expose the electrical wiring. Using a small screwdriver, install the alligator clips to the strands on this end (Fig. 10-10).

4. Strip the insulation back about an inch on the other end.

5. To test your connections, hook the open wires up to the poles of your battery. Holding the wire by the insulation, touch the alligator clips together. If everything is working, there will be a spark.

E. Launching your Gnome

1. Once the Gnome and launcher are completed, you are ready to install an engine. For smaller playgrounds, it is recommended that you use the 1/2A3-2T motor. These are great for beginners, and the rocket won't get lost as easily.

The father of space flight

10-10 *The electrical wire is equipped with two small "alligator" clips.*

2. Follow the instructions, and push the engine up into the body of the rocket.

3. Insert the igniter as shown (Fig. 10-11).

4. Insert an igniter plug of a "spit-wad" into the open end. This keeps the igniter in place.

5. Push the igniter in so it touches the propellant.

6. Bend the wires so that they are perpendicular to the motor.

7. Put the rocket on the launcher by sliding it down the wire rod. The launch lug will fit the rod perfectly.

8. The fins now rest on the square board.

9. Make sure the long electrical cord is not connected to the battery.

10. Using the alligator clips, carefully connect them to the two wires of the igniter.

11. Now string the electrical cord away from rocket.

12. Have all bystanders behind you.

13. Hook one electrical wire lead to the negative pole of the lantern battery.

14. Look around and make sure the wind is calm.

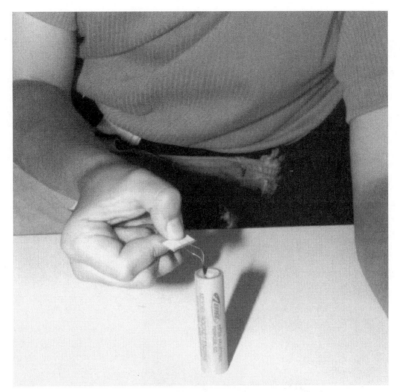

10-11 *Jennifer shows how the igniter is inserted into the Estes model rocket engine. A plug will hold it in place.*

15. Check to make sure that no one is going to be hit by the rocket model when it flies.

16. Speaking loudly enough for all bystanders to hear, start the countdown from 10, then 9 . . . (Fig. 10-12).

17. When it is safe, touch the other wire to the positive pole of the battery. This will cause the igniter to glow, and the heat will make the propellant fire.

18. The rocket should fly straight up to an altitude of about 400 feet.

19. The rocket comes down with a streamer to slow its descent and to help you find it.

20. The Gnome will fly again and again . . . Happy flying!

F. Investigations

1. Observe your rocket carefully. Does the parachute come out at the top of the flight, before, or after? Can you figure out what causes the parachute to deploy?

10-12
Rockets are a blast!

2. Time your rocket on the way up and on the way down. Are the two times equal? Why?

3. Time how long the rocket is in the air during each launch. Is the time always the same? If you observe differences in the times, think about what might cause them.

4. Mark the landing points of several launches. Are they always at the same distance from the launch pad? Are they always in the same direction relative to the launch pad? Think about what might cause any differences.

5. Read in chapter 11 about how rockets fly.

Also recommended

More project ideas!

1. *ROCKETS, A Physical Science Teacher's Guide with Activities.* Students, teachers, and parents will find this booklet to be an outstanding resource on rocketry . . . and it's free. It contains an excellent capsule of rocket history; a unit on rocket principles; practical rocketry theory with clear illustrations; models and classroom projects for everyone—such as a Hero engine, a rocket pinwheel, a rocket car, a water rocket, a 2-liter soda-pop-bottle rocket, a Newton car, paper rockets, a pencil rocket, and two-balloon

"multistage" rocket. Then it lists NASA's Educational Materials, Educational Satellite Videoconferences, NASA Select Television resources, and a Teacher Resource Center Network. The publication was in 1993, so it's up to date. Ask for *ROCKETS, A Physical Science Teacher's Guide*, #EP291. Write: Center Education Program Officer, Public Affairs Office (AP-4), NASA Johnson Space Center, Houston, TX 77058.

2. *Education Materials Publications*, by Estes Industries. Estes, the famous rocket manufacturer, has a tremendous selection of educational materials for parents and teachers. Titles include such publications as: *Model Rocketry Technical Manual*; *Alpha Book of Model Rocketry*; *Estes Guide for Aerospace Club*; *Projects in Model Rocketry*; *Model Rocketry Study Guide*; *Elementary Mathematics of Model Rockets*; *Estes Educator News*; *Industrial Arts Teachers Manual for Model Rocketry*; *Camp Leader's Model Rocketry Manual*, and more.

   These publications can be purchased from Estes. It is recommended that you order the most current free catalog of educational material and choose from their ever-expanding selection. Write: Educational Materials Catalog, Estes Industries, 1295 H Street, Penrose, Colorado 81240.

3. Quest Aerospace Educational Products. Yes, there is another company in the model rocket business. Quest has a beautiful line of models and a program for teachers and classroom projects. Dr. Ben says check this company out . . . they have good stuff!" Write Mr. Dane Boles, Quest Aerospace Educ. Products, 519 W. Lone Cactus Dr. Phoenix, AZ 85027 or phone them at 602-582-3438.

Classroom connections
A. Science

1. Demonstrate the RamRocket for the students. You will need to try it out a few times first so that you know what to expect. If the weather and space allow, an outdoor launch is much more impressive than indoors. Let the students propose explanations for what makes the rocket fly. Most students will suggest that it is somehow related to the air in the launcher pushing the rocket, and indeed it is. When you hold the rocket on while closing the launcher, you are forcing the air in the tube into a much smaller space. This increases the air pressure inside the tube and the force being exerted by the air particles on the tube walls and the rocket. When you release the rocket, this force pushes the rocket in whatever direction the launcher is pointed. In an indoor launch in which you don't hold the rocket down, the explanation is the same, but the force never gets to be as large, so the rocket doesn't go as far. As soon as the pressure builds up enough to overcome friction between the rocket and tube and the rocket's weight, it takes off. In either case, if you close the launcher too slowly, the air is able to escape around the edges of the rocket before the pressure builds up very much.

2. The RamRocket is a good device to use for an experiment in projectile motion. It is often puzzling to students that firing something horizontally is

not the way to make it travel the greatest horizontal distance. Do an experiment in which you fire the rocket at different angles and measure the distance between launching point and landing point. You might want to draw a large protractor on posterboard to assist in measuring the launch angles. On the moon, where we don't have to worry about air resistance, 45 degrees would give the greatest horizontal distance (often called range). Here on Earth, friction with the air can slow the lightweight rocket quite a bit, so you will probably get something less than 45 degrees for the maximum range. Discuss with the students why tilting the launcher upwards helps the rocket go further. This might seem strange because you are decreasing the horizontal speed as you cause the rocket to move upwards as well as outwards. However, because you are causing the rocket to go up and then come back down, you have increased the amount of time it stays in the air, giving it a chance to move further away from the launch point. Thus there is a tradeoff. As you increase the angle, you decrease the horizontal speed, but you increase the time in the air. The horizontal distance traveled is the product of these two quantities. Initially, as you increase the angle the increased time more than makes up for the decreased speed, but eventually the decreased speed wins. Think about the limiting case—firing straight up. Then you have no horizontal speed and no horizontal distance traveled. Somewhere in the middle angles, a maximum effect is produced. A more detailed explanation and other experiment ideas can be found in *Teaching Physics with Toys* by Taylor, Poth, and Portman.

3. Launching the Estes rocket will be a very exciting activity for your class, but be sure to discuss safety issues with your principal beforehand. You might want to pursue some of the ideas under "Investigations" with your students. Be sure to discuss how rockets work.

B. Mathematics

1. This a great place to review angles and angle measurements with your students if you do either the projectile motion experiment above or the investigation related to the direction of the Gnome landing point relative to its launch point.

2. Make a line graph of the projectile motion data by plotting the angle versus the horizontal distance traveled. Discuss with the students the advantages of graphs in helping us make sense of data.

C. Social studies

1. Using a piece of 8½-inch × 11-inch writing paper, fold it in half, lengthwise. At the top of the first side, write the name Robert Goddard. At the top of the second half, write the name Wernher von Braun, a German scientist who also made important contributions to rocket science. Use encyclopedias and other references to research these two men and write facts to compare their lives.

2. Read *Rocket! How a Toy Launched the Space Age* by Richard Maurer. This book is an interesting mix of history and science. Much more than a biography of Goddard, it examines the scientific process in which the

solution of a series of small problems finally leads to the larger goal, the newest breakthrough builds on the previous ones, and as much is learned from our mistakes as our successes. This book really makes history come alive.

3. It seems appropriate to end our studies of flight with the Space Shuttle Program. While women were excluded from both the Mercury and Apollo programs, the Space Shuttle Program finally made space travel a realistic goal for girls and boys. Junior-high students will find *Women in Space: Reaching the Last Frontier* by Carole Briggs to be quite readable. The training and achievements of 14 women in the Space Shuttle Program are described. In addition, the reader is introduced to several women from other countries who have traveled in space.

D. Language arts

1. Upper elementary students will enjoy learning more about Robert Goddard in *The Boy Who Dreamed of Rockets* by Robert Quackenbush. *Robert Hutching Goddard: Pioneer of Rocketry and Space Flight* by Suzanne Coil and *Wernher von Braun: Space Visionary and Rocket Engineer* by Spangenberg and Moser, both from the Makers of Modern Science series, are excellent biographies for older students to read.

2. Dr. Goddard was a scientist who refused to give up trying to develop his ideas. Even when other people didn't believe in him, he quietly continued to work. Write a one-page essay entitled, "Stick With It, It's a Great Idea." Share your essay with someone else.

3. Using rhyming words, write a four-stanza poem about rockets. Some words you might use for your poem might include blastoff, launch, fire, countdown, splashdown, etc.

4. Design a poster to advertise the first rocket launch. Think creatively and develop your own slogan.

5. Former Mercury Astronaut and current U.S. Senator John Glenn once said, "The more I see, the more impressed I am not with how much we know, but with how tremendous the areas are that are as yet unexplored." Choose one of the following related topics for discussion or research:
   a. The first astronauts who looked back to the Earth were amazed at what they saw. The Apollo moon missions gave us the first view of our planet as a whole. Have you ever seen something really amazing? Discuss this with a class group or a parent. You might want to write about it.
   b. Choose some area of the Earth that you would like to explore. Find out as much as you can about this area. Why did you choose this area? What interests you about it? How would you go about exploring it? What would you do to record your exploration?
   c. Choose a topic on the current frontier of science, such as the search for a cure for AIDS or for dark matter in the universe or for understanding of how ocean currents affect global temperatures. Read about it and share what you learned.

The father of space flight

How they fly 11

In order to understand what happens when things move through the air, we must first know something about air. The air around you is made up of billions of tiny particles that are constantly moving in all directions. Imagine a little cube that is about the size of your thumbnail on each side. The air in that little cube is made up of so many little particles that you and I can't even imagine a number that big—more than a billion billion billion. Yet these particles are so tiny that most of the cube is still empty space. These particles are moving very rapidly in all directions and are constantly bumping into one another. A typical particle in the air in your room is moving at around 500 meters per second. That's fast! That is so fast that, if it didn't  bump into something first (like a wall), it would travel the length of five football fields every second. Keep this picture of lots of tiny, fast-moving particles in mind as we go on.

The particles in the air are continually bumping into things: walls, chairs, each other, you, and anything else in the room. We need to think about what happens when they hit a wall or anything else. First, what happens when you throw a shoe at the wall? You hear a thud, and if you threw it hard enough, you might see a dent. In physics terms, we would say the shoe exerted a force on the wall. The wall also exerted a force on the shoe. We know it did because the shoe changed its direction of motion. It turned around and came back at you. Changes in motion require forces to produce them. That is one of the laws of physics that was discovered several hundred years ago. Another law of physics, called Newton's Third Law, says that if one object (the shoe) exerts a force on another object (the wall), then the second object (the wall) will exert a force of the same size, but in the opposite direction, back on the first object (the shoe). Gee, that's a lot of words. Stop here and think hard about it a minute because it will be important to understanding flight. If my hand pushes on the table, the table pushes back on me. The force of the table on my hand is what keeps my hand from just continuing to move on through the table.

Now let's go back to thinking about those tiny particles. The same thing happens when they hit the wall that happened when the shoe hit the wall. They exert a force on the wall, and the wall exerts a force back on them. These forces are tiny because the particles are so small. But because there are so many, many of them, these tiny forces can add up to be quite important. You might be wondering at this point why you don't feel the particles bouncing off of your body all the time. Remember, they are moving in all directions, so particles are hitting you from all directions at once. If you want to feel these particles hitting you, just go stand in the wind. In a wind, whether natural or created by a fan, the particles are no longer moving equally in all directions. There are more particles moving in the direction of the wind than in other directions. So you feel a force from that direction.

Okay, so now you have a mental picture of air as lots of little tiny particles moving around very rapidly in all directions, bouncing off things and exerting forces on them. There is one effect of these forces that you need to know about before we tackle flight. Cut a strip about an inch wide from a sheet of paper. Hold one end of the paper just below your mouth and blow across it. Notice how it rises. Before you blew, the particles in the air above and below the air were continually bouncing off and exerting forces on it. But the forces on the top were equal to the forces on the bottom, so nothing happened. When you blew across it, you replaced the particles on top that were moving equally in all directions with ones that were mostly moving outward across the paper. So fewer particles were moving in the right direction to bump into the top of the paper. But nothing changed on the bottom of the paper, so now there is a bigger force on the bottom of the paper than on the top. Aha, that's why the paper rose. The forces from the particles on the bottom pushed it up because the particles on the top weren't pushing down as hard as they used to be. When things like airplanes are moving through the air, the same thing happens. It doesn't matter whether it is the air that is moving, as when you blew over the paper, or whether the airplane is moving through the air. The result is the same (Fig. 11-1).

If you would like to do some more experiments with air and learn more about air in the process, take a look at *Air* by Brenda Walpole or *Air, Wind and Flight* by Pam Robson. Both these books are chock full of experiments and projects.

Kites

There are three forces on a flying kite: the force of gravity, the force of the air, and the force applied by the string. If the kite is in stable flight, these three forces are balanced. That means they add up to zero. If they didn't, then the kite would move in the direction of the total force. The directions of these three

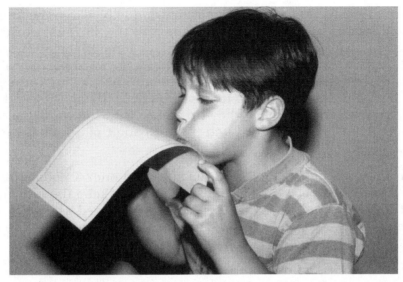

11-1 *When David blows over the wing-shaped paper, it rises.*

Side view of kite

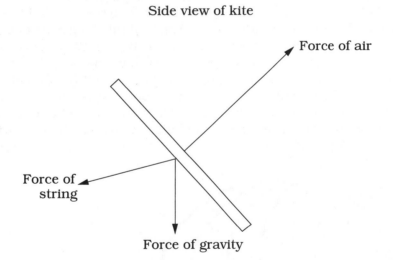

Force of air

Force of string

Force of gravity

11-2 *When a kite is in stable flight, the three forces exerted by the air, gravity, and the string balance each other.*

forces are shown in Fig. 11-2. Gravity is, of course, straight down. The force exerted by the string pulls in the direction of the string and changes with the position of the kite. Newton's Third Law is the key to understanding the direction of the force the air exerts on the kite. Remember that we fly kites in a wind. So all those little particles are moving in a generally horizontal direction. They hit the surface of the kite and bounce off. If the kite flew straight up and down (like a wall), the force of the kite on the particles would just turn them around. However, since the kite sits in the air at an angle, it pushes them down as well. Picture a pool ball striking the wall of the pool table and bouncing off at an angle. That is what the particles of air do when they hit the kite. Relative to the direction from which the wind is blowing, the kite pushes down and backwards on the air. That tells us that the air must at the same time be pushing up and forward on the kite. This force is sometimes discussed in two parts. The upward part is called *lift* and the forward part is called *drag*. The lift part of the force is what "lifts" the kite into the air and keeps gravity from pulling it back down. How big this force is depends on the wind speed, the area of the kite, and the angle the kite makes with the wind (called *angle of attack*). A kite will fly in a position such that the angle of attack is just right to make all the forces on the kite cancel out.

What about tails on kites? Why didn't our kite need one? Tails on kites help provide stability. The force of the air on the tail helps keep the kite facing into the wind. This is important because if the kite gets turned sideways, so that most of the air just goes right by it, then it loses its lift and falls. The added weight at the bottom also helps keep the kite in the proper position. Our kite didn't need a tail because its shape provides all the stability it needs.

Hot-air balloons

A hot-air balloon rises because the air inside is warmer than the surrounding air. Imagine an inflated beach ball in a swimming pool. Take the ball down to the bottom, and it jumps right back to the surface. If you could fill the ball with sand instead of air, it wouldn't float. The ball filled with air is lighter than the ball filled with sand. We could also say that the ball filled with air has a smaller density (less mass in the same volume) than the ball filled with sand. Density determines whether something sinks or floats. If the density of the object is less than the density of water, it will float; if it is greater, it will sink. This is called the *principle of buoyancy*. Think of cold air being like the water and hot air being like the air inside of the ball. The hot-air balloon will float in the cold outside air (Fig. 11-3).

11-3
The hot-air ballon floats in the more dense, cold air surrounding it.

You might be wondering why there is a difference in the density of hot and cold air. When the air inside the balloon is heated, the particles start to move faster and they hit the inside of the balloon harder and more often. This increased force on the inside of the balloon makes it expand. This has the effect of allowing the particles to move further apart. Some of the particles even escape out the bottom of the balloon. Since there are now fewer particles and they are spread out more, the air in the balloon is now less dense than it was. The density of the hot air can be low enough that the density of the air plus the balloon is less than that of the cold air outside. Thus the balloon floats.

Shortly after the Montgolfier brothers started flying their balloons, another Frenchman devised a balloon that used hydrogen gas rather than air. The hydrogen did not have to be heated because hydrogen is naturally less dense than air. The particles in hydrogen gas are much lighter than the particles in air. Since the hydrogen did not have to be heated, this solved the problems the Montgolfiers had with fires. However, it was still dangerous because hydrogen can very easily explode. Modern-day blimps use helium instead of hydrogen. Helium is more dense, so the balloons can't go as high, but helium is much safer.

Birds

Birds are wonderful creatures and they are built to fly. They have light bodies and powerful muscles. How birds use their wings is actually quite complicated, and different kinds of birds use different motions. However, there are a few things they have in common. When a bird flies, its powerful muscles push its wings downward against the air underneath. The air then pushes up on the wings with exactly the same size force. (There's Newton's Third Law again.) This force is big enough to lift the bird into the air. Once in the air, the bird must continue to move its wings at least part of the time so that the air will push upward hard enough to cancel out the force of gravity, which pulls down on the bird. Humans will never be able to fly like birds because our muscles aren't strong enough to produce a downward force on the air that is larger than the force of gravity on us (our weight). Birds can do it because their weight is so small. In relation to their weight, birds muscles are much stronger than ours (Fig. 11-4).

11-4
The bird's wings push down and back on the air, so the air pushes up and forward on the bird.

So that's what keeps a bird up, but how does it move forward? There are lots of bones and muscles in a bird's wing, so it has good control of the position of its feathers. As the wing pushes down, the bird twists the outer portion of the wing so that it pushes backwards as well. (You know what's coming next.) That means the air pushes forward on the bird. You might be wondering how the bird gets its wing back in position for another downstroke without exerting an upward force on the air and having the air push it down, canceling out the effect of the downstroke. On the upstroke the bird changes the position of its wings and feathers. The wings sweep back and partially fold up so the amount of surface area that contacts the air is much smaller. The feathers can also be lifted or twisted so that it is easy for the air to just slip by them. This greatly reduces the force the wing exerts on the air.

Once the bird is moving through the air, the curved shape of the wing is also important to providing an upward force to help keep it there, just like it is for airplanes. That is why birds don't have to flap as hard once they are flying as they do taking off. We will talk more about this when we get to airplanes.

When a bird wants to land, it can descend by gliding to the ground. It can control the speed with which it comes down by partially extending its wings. If they are fully extended, it will glide down very slowly. If they are completely folded against its body, it will drop rapidly, just like when you drop a rock. You might have seen this sort of dive when watching some kinds of birds dive after fish. When it is time to land, birds might flap their wings frantically while turning them to present a large surface area to the wind. The air will push backwards on the bird, just like when you hold your hand out the car window. Watch a bird land sometime, and you will see this happen. It is like they are trying to fly backwards but gently settling to the earth.

Airplanes

Let's review. A bird's wings push down and backward on the air. This causes the air to push up and forward on the bird. The upward part of the force is sometimes called "lift" and the forward part is called "thrust."

In an airplane, these two forces are provided separately rather than together. Sir George Cayley might have been the first person to realize that this would be necessary for a successful airplane flight. In modern airplanes, the wings are important to the "lift" force, but unlike birds, an airplane's wings do not provide "thrust." The engine and propeller create the thrust (Fig. 11-5).

To understand how lift is created by an airplane's wings, we need to go back and remember the blowing across the sheet of paper experiment. Back in the section on air, we said airplanes worked the same way. As the airplane moves through the air, the air molecules don't hit the wing as often as they would if the wing was stationary, just like blowing across the sheet of paper. However, there is a problem here, which you might have already noticed if you are thinking really hard. When we did the sheet of paper experiment, we only blew across the top of the paper, so particles of air were hitting the bottom of the air just like normal. But both the top and bottom of the airplane wing have air moving across them, so the force should be lowered both places. There should be no larger force on the bottom to push the wing up like it pushed the paper

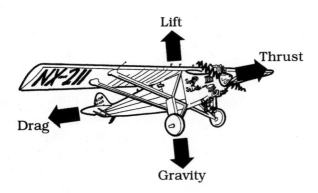

11-5
There are four forces acting on an airplane in flight.

up. The thing that gets us out of this difficulty is the shape of the wing. There is an upward curve on the top of the wing, while the bottom of the wing is more or less flat. It turns out that this causes the particles of air traveling across the top of the wing to move faster than the ones moving across the bottom of the wing. Why the particles move across the curved top faster than the flat bottom is pretty complicated. You're just going to have to trust us on this one. They really do move faster on top. This means that the particles push down on the top of the wing with a smaller force than they push up on the bottom of the wing, so when we add the upward and downward forces together, the sum is an upward or "lift" force.

If you look closely at the shape of a propeller, you will see that it resembles an airplane wing. You can even think of it as a rotating wing. As the engine turns the propeller, "lift" is produced just like with the wing, but since the propeller is turned sideways, the force is horizontal, not vertical. This force, now called "thrust," pushes the plane forward. Think about standing in front of a fan on a hot day. The fan throws air toward you. It is exerting a force on the air to move air forward, so the air must be exerting an opposite force on the fan. If we mounted the fan on a cart (or a couple of skateboards), the cart would move in the opposite direction from the air. In the case of the airplane, the propellers are shaped so that they push the air toward the back of the plane. The air then pushes the plane forward (Fig. 11-6).

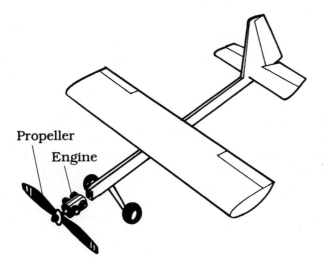

11-6
The rotating propeller causes the air to push the plane forward. This force is called thrust.

The Wright brothers were not the first to get an airplane off the ground, but they were the first to be able to control their plane. Controlling an aircraft can be tricky because you must do it without upsetting the crucial balance between lift and gravity, which keeps the plane aloft. Modern airplanes, and most gliders, have a set of control "surfaces" that allow the pilot to change direction. First let's look at the ailerons. These are a set of hinged flaps on the back edge of a plane's wings. If the ailerons are raised, the air slows down over the wing and there is less lift. If the ailerons are lowered, the air slows down below the wing and there is more lift. The ailerons are used to turn the plane. When the pilot wants to turn, the aileron on one wing is lowered and the one on the other wing is raised. This increases the lift on one wing, so it rises, and decreases the lift on the other, so it drops. This motion is called a *roll*. If the left wing is the one that dropped, then the plane will turn left. Dropping the right wing causes the plane to turn right. This is called *banking* the plane. You have probably experienced this on your bicycle. If you are going fast enough, you just lean the bike in the direction you want to go. If you lean the bike to the left, it turns to the left (Fig. 11-7).

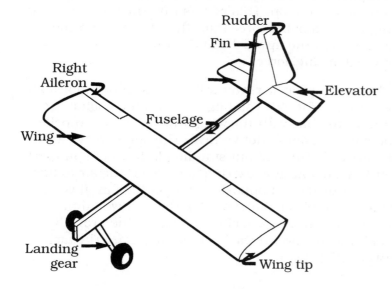

11-7
The ailerons, elevators, and rudder allow the airplane to make turns and change its attitude.

The other two kinds of control surfaces are on the tail of the plane. The tail has two parts: a horizontal stabilizer (it looks like a small wing) and a vertical fin. The rudder is a hinged flap on the back of the fin. The rudder can be moved to the right or left so that it sticks out into the air moving past the plane. If the rudder is moved to the left, the air hitting it exerts a force on it, which pushes the tail of the plane to the right. The whole plane pivots, swinging the nose to the left, and the plane turns left. Pilots use a combination of rudder and aileron control to make turns. The other control surface is the elevators, which are like the ailerons, but on the horizontal part of the tail rather than the wing. If the elevators are lowered, this increases the lift on the tail, so the tail rises and the nose drops. This causes the plane to dive. If the elevators are raised, just the opposite happens.

Gliders

With the exception of the rubber-band-powered plane in chapter 6, all our airplanes are really gliders. They do not have engines to create forward thrust. You had to get them started by throwing them.

First let's talk about real gliders, then we'll come back to our models. Since a glider does not have an engine or a propeller, it must be towed by another airplane. The "tow-plane" pulls the glider up to a certain height, or altitude, where it can be released. Once it has released the glider, the tow-plane returns to the airport while the glider continues to fly. The glider continues on with whatever forward speed it had when the tow-plane released it. The long, curved wings provide lift just like an airplane's wings do, but usually this force is smaller than the force of gravity pulling down on the glider, so it gradually starts to descend.

There are currents of air, much like wind, that go straight up from the ground. These currents are called *thermals*. When a glider gets in one of these thermals, it can be pushed upward away from the earth. Glider pilots say they are getting "lift" from these thermals. The pilots stay in the rising columns of air to go higher and higher. Eventually, the thermal cools and no longer provides lift. When this occurs, the glider starts slowly downward again. Glider pilots will sometimes spend hours going from one thermal to another to stay aloft. The sport of gliding is called "soaring."

You might be wondering how our model gliders get their lift since they don't have curved wings and there probably weren't any thermals around. To understand our models, we need to think about several different things. First, think about what happens when you drop a sheet of paper or a feather. It drifts very slowly to the ground. This happens because it has a very small weight and a large surface area. The large surface area means the air exerts a large upward force on the paper as it falls. This force is a kind of friction. Imagine dropping a marble in a jar of honey. It falls very slowly, just like the paper in the air. We don't notice this friction force when we drop a marble in the air because the force the air exerts is much smaller than the force the honey exerts. The friction with the air is only important if the object's weight is very small like the paper or feather. The larger the surface area of the object, the bigger this force is. Our gliders all had large wings and were very lightweight, so that as they drop, they experience a significant upward friction force, just like the sheet of paper.

You probably found that the glider flew better if you launched it with its nose slightly upward. This causes the particles of air to hit the wings at an angle, just like we discussed in the section on kites. This provides some lift also. If you lift the nose of the glider too high, the backward force of the air (drag) on the glider quickly slows the glider down. Take a look at the various gliders you have built. They are all very slim and flat. They present a very small forward surface area to the air to reduce the drag force. In order to produce a good, long flight with your glider, you need to balance these two effects. Point the nose up just a little to provide some lift, but not so much that the drag slows the glider down too soon.

Drag is also very important to real gliders and airplanes. The faster the airplane flies, the bigger the drag force is. That is why planes that are meant to fly very fast are always designed to be very smooth and streamlined.

While flying your gliders, you probably noticed that they didn't always behave the same way in flight. Sometimes you got a nice smooth, almost "lazy" flight. Other times the glider would dive or rise rapidly and then stall. These undesirable behaviors can be caused by a number of things. If the nose is too heavy or the elevators set too low, the glider will dive. Launching the glider too slowly can also cause the glider to dive, but in this case it might recover and level out. As the plane dives, it picks up speed (just like any falling object will speed up as it falls). This increased speed of the air over the wing increases the lift. If the glider is properly balanced, this increased lift might be enough to produce a stable flight.

If the tail is too heavy, the elevators are set too high, or it is launched too fast, the glider will rise rapidly. As it rises it slows down. This results in decreased lift both because of decreased airspeed and increased angle of attack. It will eventually "stall" when the lift drops to less than the downward force of gravity. Once it stalls, it usually turns its nose down and drops. As it falls, it picks up speed and might level out again. Sometimes a wavy motion is produced as it rises and falls several times before settling into a steady flight. Real planes can also be stalled if they rise too steeply.

Rockets

Over the years, there has been much misinformation about how rockets fly. So much so that many people told Goddard that his rocket could never work in space where there is no air. We'll come back to this after we know how rockets do work.

I want you to do what scientists call a "thought experiment." You are going to imagine doing an experiment and think about what the results would be. Many times, when scientists do thought experiments it is because the experiment can't really be performed. In this case, you really could do it, but you are busy reading this book right now. Imagine putting on your roller skates, grabbing a basketball, and going down to the playground. Stand on a level, paved area and throw the basketball hard, straight out in front of you. What happened? Put your imagination to work. Think about other experiences you have had on roller skates. You rolled backwards. If you threw it harder or used a heavier object, then your backwards speed would be even greater. Remember Newton's Third Law. You pushed the basketball forward, so the basketball pushed you backward. You didn't move as fast as the basketball because your mass is much bigger than the ball's.

Rockets work the same way. As the exhaust from the burning fuel moves backwards out of the rocket, the rocket is pushed forward. The rocket moves slowly compared to the exhaust gas because its mass is much bigger. In our balloon rocket, we just have air escaping instead of exhaust gases, but the principle is the same. If you have gone hunting and fired a rifle, you have experienced this physics principle up close. The rifle pushes the bullet forward, and the bullet pushes the rifle backwards into your shoulder. The rifle is like the rocket, and the bullet is like the exhaust gas.

In the past, many people have used Newton's Third Law incorrectly when trying to understand rockets. They thought the air outside the rocket was important. Instead of looking at the forces between the rocket and the exhaust gas, they looked at the forces between the exhaust gases and the air. They said the exhaust gases push on the air beneath the rocket, and this air then pushes back against the exhaust gases. Somehow the exhaust gases transmit this force back to the rocket. Based on this explanation, they concluded that rockets needed air to push on and so could not possibly work in space. So many people told Goddard that his idea couldn't possibly work that he began to doubt if it would. He set up an experiment to test whether a rocket could work in a vacuum. He put a small rocket in a long pipe and then used a pump to take all the air out of the pipe. He fired the rocket. Not only did it work, but it worked better than before! Now that there wasn't any air in the way, the rocket engine could force the exhaust gases out even faster. Remember: the rocket pushes on the exhaust gases and the gases push on the rocket. The outside air isn't needed at all; in fact, it even gets in the way.

What if I want to know more?

We have just barely begun to explore the science of flight (sometimes called aerodynamics). If you would like to learn more, you might want to start out by reading *Up, Up, and Away: The Science of Flight* by D. Darling or *Airborne: The Search for the Secret of Flight* by R. Maurer. After that, well, who knows where you'll wind up. After all, the sky's not the limit anymore.

Resources

Where do you write when you want to find out more about aviation and space-related subjects? This has been a problem for students, parents, and teachers—until now! This appendix tells you where to get all kinds of materials, and most of these materials are free!

A letter by you, to them

Figure A-1 on page 132 is a form letter for you to write for materials. All you have to do is copy the letter with your information inserted and mail it to the company. Big companies often have a special office to help people with information. The office is called public relations or public affairs. A letter addressed directly to the proper office will get it to the right person faster. It's easy because all you have to do is use this form letter, insert their company address and your information. Good luck.

Associations

4-H Aerospace Education
National 4-H Program
U.S. Dept. of Agriculture
Room 38605
Washington, DC 20250

(An outreach program for projects in aviation and space)

Aerospace Industries Association of America, Inc.
1250 Eye St. NW
Washington, DC 20005

(Information on aerospace manufacturing, including aircraft, missiles, spacecraft, helicopters, and equipment)

Air Force Office of Youth Relations
Kelly AFB
TX 78241-5000

(Information about the Air Force)

Your name
Your address
Your city, state, and zip code

Date of the letter

Office of Public Affairs
Company name
Company address
Company city, state, and zip code

Dear Sir:

My name is _____ and I am a student at (the name of your school) _____. I am doing a project and would like to have your help. I found your address in the book, <u>Let's Build Airplanes and Rockets</u> by Dr. Ben Millspaugh and Dr. Beverley Taylor.

The subject of my project is _____. I have to have my project finished and handed in by _____ (the date your assignment is due if doing this for a teacher/class).

I was wondering if you would please send me _____ (talk to your teacher and make a precise request for information, photos, brochures, catalogs, prices, and the like).

If you have any materials that you think might help with my project, I would appreciate receiving them. Thank you for helping.

Sincerely,
(Your signature)

A-1 *Your letter.*

Air Line Pilots Association
1625 Massachusetts Ave. NW
Washington, DC 20036

(Education, safety, and pilot career information)

Air Traffic Control Association
220 N. 14th St., Suite 410
Arlington, VA 22201

(Information on national air traffic control)

Air Transport Association of America
Public Relations Committee
1709 New York Ave. NW
Washington, DC 20006

(Information about airlines and airline-related industries)

Aircraft Electronics Association
P.O. Box 1981
Independence, MO 64055

(Information about aircraft radios and navigation electronics)

Resources

Aircraft Owners and Pilots Association
421 Aviation Way
Frederick, MD 21701

(Information on general aviation regulations, safety, and community airports)

American Helicopter Society, Inc.
217 North Washington St.
Alexandria, VA 22314

(Information about helicopters and related subjects)

American Institute of Aeronautics & Astronautics
370 L'Enfant Promenade SW
Washington, DC 20024

(Educational material on aeronautics and astronautics)

Animal Air Transportation Association
P.O. Box 441110
Fort Washington, MD 20744

(Information on the methods and services for national and international air transportation of animals)

Aviation Distributors and Manufacturers Association
1900 Arch St.
Philadelphia, PA 19103

(Information on aviation products, distributors, and educational materials related to aviation)

Aviation Maintenance Foundation, Inc.
P.O. Box 2826
Redmond, WA 98073

(Vocational guidance, books, and technical materials)

Cessna Aircraft Company
Air Age Education
P.O. Box 1521
Wichita, KS 67201

(Information about aviation, the company, and company products)

Challenger Center for Space Science Education
Education Department
1101 King St., Suite 190
Alexandria, VA 22314

(Information about space and space-related subjects)

Civil Air Patrol
Building 714
Maxwell AFB, AL 33112-5872

(Aerospace education programs and materials. CAP is an auxiliary of the United States Air Force)

Experimental Aircraft Association
Educational Division
Wittman Field
Oshkosh, WI 54903-3086

(Information on building airplanes, kitplanes, sport aviation, antique and war plane restoration, aviation camps, and summer academy programs)

Federal Aviation Administration
Aviation Education APA-100
800 Independence Ave. SW
Washington, DC 20591

(Information on all facets of aviation. The FAA offers a tremendous amount of aviation educational material, as well as films and audiovisual aids for teachers)

General Aviation Manufacturers Association
1400 K St. NW, Suite 801
Washington, DC 20005

(Information on general aviation statistics, learning to fly, teaching, and the manufacture of airplanes)

Jeppesen-Sanderson
55 Inverness Drive East
Englewood, CO 80112

(Textbooks, overhead projection materials, videocassettes, and more about learning to fly)

NASA Educational Affairs Division
Code XEO, NASA Headquarters
Washington, DC 20546

(Information about space-related subjects)

National Aeronautics and Space Administration
Educational Programs Office
600 Independence Ave.
Washington, DC 20548

(Information on career opportunities and educational materials relating to space)

National Agricultural Aviation Association
115 D St. SE, Suite 103
Washington, DC 20003

(Materials and information on agricultural aviation)

National Air and Space Museum
Public Relations Department
7th St. and Independence Ave. SW
Washington, DC 20560

(Information about aviation and space history)

National Air Transportation Association
4226 King St.
Alexandria, VA 22302

(Information on airport service organizations, air charter, and flight training)

National Association of Air Traffic Specialists
4780 Corridor Place
Beltsville, MD 20705

(Information on careers in air traffic control)

National Association of State Aviation Officials
Metro Plaza One, Suite 505
8401 Colesville Road
Silver Spring, MD 20910

(Information about state aviation departments and materials that might be available)

National Space Society
922 Pennsylvania Ave. SE
Washington, DC 20003

(Information about space-related subjects)

National Transportation Safety Board
Office of Public Affairs
800 Independence Ave. SW
Washington, DC 20591

(Information on air traffic safety and accident investigation)

Soaring Society of America, Inc.
P.O. Box E
Hobbs, NM 88241

(Information about gliders and soaring)

The Ninety-Nines, Inc.
Will Rogers World Airport
P.O. Box 59965
Oklahoma City, OK 73159

(An organization of women pilots that helps promote aviation through national activities)

The Young Astronaut Council
Suite 800, 1211 Connecticut Ave., NW
Washington, DC 20036

(Information about the council's youth astronaut program)

Unique Patchwork Kites
Attn: Scott R. Skinner
Suite 406, Alamo Building
128 S. Tejon St.
Colorado Springs, CO 80903

United States Hang Glider Association
P.O. Box 8300
Colorado Springs, CO 80933

United States Space Foundation
P.O. Box 1838
Colorado Springs, CO 80901

(Information about space-related subjects)

Bibliography

1990 Guiness Book of World Records, Donald McFarlan, Editor, Sterling Publishing, New York, 1989, ISBN 0-8069-5790-5.

53½ Things that Changed the World and Some that Didn't!, David West and Stephen Parker, Millbrook Press, Brookfield, Connecticut, 1992, ISBN 1-56294-894-6.

Air, Fun with Science series, Brenda Walpole, Warwick Press, New York, 1987, ISBN 0-531-19024-2.

Airborne: The Search for the Secret of Flight, Richard Maurer, Simon and Schuster, New York, 1990, ISBN 0-671-69422-7.

Air, Wind and Flight, Science Workshop series, Pam Robson, Gloucester Press, New York, 1992, ISBN 0-531-17375-5.

At the Controls: Women in Aviation, Carole Briggs, Lerner Publications, Minneapolis, 1991, ISBN 0-8225-1593-8.

Before the Wright Brothers, Don Berliner, Lerner Publications, Minneapolis, 1990, ISBN 0-8225-1588-1.

Black Eagles: African Americans in Aviation, Jim Haskins, Scholastic Inc., New York, 1995, ISBN 0-590-45912-0.

Breakthrough: Women in Aviation, Elizabeth Simpson Smith, Walker and Company, New York, 1981, ISBN 0-8027-6433-9.

Chuck Yeager, the first man to fly faster than sound, People of Distinction series, Timothy R. Gaffney, Childrens Press, Chicago, 1986, ISBN 0-516-03223-2.

Chuck Yeager, the man who broke the sound barrier, Nancy Smiler Levinson, Walker, New York, 1988, ISBN 0-8027-6781-8.

Eureka! It's an Airplane, Jeanne Bendick, Millbrook Press, Brookfield, Connecticut, 1992, ISBN 1-56294-058-9.

Flight, Robert Burleigh, Philomel Books, New York, 1991, ISBN 0-399-22272-3.

Flight: Fliers and Flying Machines, Timelines series, David Jefferis, Franklin Watts, New York, 1991, ISBN 0-531-15233-2.

Flights of Imagination: An Introduction to Aerodynamics, Wayne Hosking, National Science Teachers Association, Washington, DC, 1990, ISBN 0-87355-067-6.

Flying Free: America's First Black Aviators, Philip Hart, Lerner Publications, Minneapolis, 1992, ISBN 0-8225-1598-9.

History's Timeline: A 40,000 Year Chronology of Civilization, Jean Cooke, Ann Kramer, and Theodore Rowland-Entwistle, Crescent Books, New York, 1981, ISBN 0-517-34000-3.

How to Make and Fly Paper Airplanes, Ralph S. Barnaby, Four Winds Press, New York, 1968, ISBN 0-590-07102-5.

How to Think Like a Scientist: Answering Questions by the Scientific Method, Stephen P. Kramer, Thomas Y. Crowell Books, New York, 1987, ISBN 0-690-04563-8.

Ladybirds: The Untold Story of Women Pilots in America, Henry Holden, Black Hawk Publishing, Mt. Freedom, NJ, 1991, ISBN 1-87963-011-7.

Leonardo Da Vinci: Artist, Inventor and Scientist of the Renaissance, Masters of Art series, Peter Bedrick Books, New York, 1994, ISBN 0-87226-313-4.

Lindbergh, Chris Demarest, Crown Publishers, New York, 1993, ISBN 0-517-58718-1.

Lindbergh Alone, Brendan Gill, Harcourt Brace Jovanovich, New York, 1977, ISBN 0-15-152401-7.

Mothers of Invention: from the bra to the bomb, forgotten women and their unforgettable ideas, Ethlie Ann Vare and Greg Ptacek, Morrow Publishing, NY, 1988, ISBN 0-688-06464-7.

National Science Education Standards, National Academy Press, Washington, D.C., 1996, ISBN 0-309-05326-9.

Pioneers of Flight, Tales of Courage series Brian Williams, Steck Vaughn Library, Austin, 1990, ISBN 0-8114-2755-2.

Queen Bess: Daredevil Aviator, Doris Rich, Smithsonian Institution Press, Washington, 1993, ISBN 1-56098-265-9.

Robert Hutchings Goddard: Pioneer of Rocketry and Space Flight, Makers of Modern Science series, Suzanne M. Coil, Facts on File, New York, 1992, ISBN 0-8160-2591-6.

Rocket! How a Toy Launched the Space Age, Richard Maurer, Crown Publishers, New York, 1995, ISBN 0-517-59628-8.

Sky Stars: The History of Women in Aviation, Ann Hodgman and Rudy Djabbaroff, Atheneum Press, New York, 1981, ISBN 0-689-30870-1.

Smithsonian Visual Timeline of Inventions, Anderly Moore, Project Editor, Dorling Kindersley Publishing, London, 1994, ISBN 1-56458-675-8.

Steven Caney's Invention Book, Steven Caney, Workman Publishing, New York, 1985, ISBN 0-89480-076-0.

Teaching Physics with Toys: Activities for Grades K-9, Beverley Taylor, James Poth and Dwight Portman, TAB Books, New York, 1995, ISBN 0-07-064721-6.

The Ancient Chinese, Lai Po Kan, Silver Burdett, Morristown, New Jersey, 1981, ISBN 0-382-06446-1.

The Ancient Far East, Just Look At series, Yonit Percival and Alastair Percival, Rouke Enterprises, Vero Beach, Florida, 1988, ISBN 0-86592-897-5.

The Boy Who Dreamed of Rockets, Robert Quackenbush, Parents' Magazine Press, New York, 1978, ISBN 0-8193-0995-8.

The Flying Balloon, Tales from History series, Cyriel Verleyen, Thomas Y. Crowell Co., New York, 1968.

The Genius of China: 3,000 year of science, discovery and invention, Rober Temple, Simon and Schuster, New York, 1986, ISBN 0-671-62028-2.

The Picture Book History of Great Inventors, Gillian Clements, Alfred A. Knopf, New York, 1993, ISBN 0-679-84788-X.

The Story of the Flight at Kitty Hawk, R. Conrad Stein, Children's Press, Chicago, 1981, ISBN 0-516-04614-4.

The Story of The Spirit of St. Louis, R. Conrad Stein, Children's Press, Chicago, 1984, ISBN 0-516-04667-5.

The Timeline of Discovery and Invention, Peter North and Philip Wilkinson, Galahad Jr. Books, New York, 1993, ISBN 0-88394-973-3.

The Ultimate Kite Book, Paul Morgan and Helene Morgan, Simon and Schuster, New York, 1992, ISBN 0-671-74443-7.

The Wright Brothers: How They Invented The Airplane, Russell Freedman, Holiday House, New York, 1991, ISBN 0-8234-0875-2.

Those Wonderful Women and Their Flying Machines, Sally Van Wagenen Keil, Rawson Wade Publishers, New York, 1979, ISBN 0-89256-066-5.

Up, Up, and Away: The Science of Flight, David Darling, Dillon Press, New York, 1991, ISBN 0-87518-479-0.

Wernher von Braun: Space Visionary and Rocket Engineer, Makers of Modern Science series, Ray Spangenburg and Diane K. Moser, Facts on File, New York, 1995, ISBN 0-8160-2924-5.

Women in Space: Reaching the Last Frontier, Carole Briggs, Lerner Publications, Minneapolis, 1988, ISBN 0-8225-1581-4.

Women of the Air, David Mondey, Silver Burdett, Morristown, NJ, 1981, ISBN 0-382-06634-0.

Women with Wings: Female Flyers in Fact and Fiction, Mary Cadogan, Academy Chicago Publishers, Chicago, 1993, ISBN 0-89733-385-3.

World History Dates, Usborne Illustrated World History Series, Jane Chisholm, Usborne Publishing, London, 1987, ISBN 0-86020-954-7.

Index